Extraterrestrial Life

New and future titles in the series include:
Alien Abductions
Angels
Atlantis
The Bermuda Triangle
The Curse of King Tut
Dragons
Dreams
ESP
The Extinction of the Dinosaurs
Fairies
Fortune-Telling
Ghosts
Haunted Houses
The Kennedy Assassination
King Arthur
The Loch Ness Monster
Pyramids
Stonehenge
UFOs
Unicorns
Vampires
Witches

The Mystery Library

Extraterrestrial Life

Don Nardo

LUCENT
BOOKS®

THOMSON
———✷———™
GALE

San Diego • Detroit • New York • San Francisco • Cleveland • New Haven, Conn. • Waterville, Maine • London • Munich

On Cover: A region of the Milky Way, Earth's galaxy. The mysterious lure of space—and the prospect that Earth may not be the only planet populated with sentient beings—continues to fascinate many.

LIBRARY OF CONGRESS CATALOGING-IN-PUBLICATION DATA

Nardo, Don, 1947–
    Extraterrestrial life / by Don Nardo.
        p. cm. — (The mystery library)
Includes bibliographical references and index.
Contents: How likely or common is extraterrestrial life? — What physical forms might extraterrestrials have? — Are extraterrestrial spacecraft visiting Earth? — the ongoing search for sentient extraterrestrials.
    ISBN 1-59018-320-7 (hardback : alk. paper)
    1. Life on other planets—Juvenile literature. [1. Extraterrestrial beings. 2. Life on other planets.] I. Title. II Series: Mystery library (Lucent Books)
    QB54.N37 2004
    576.8'39—dc22
                                                                            2003017748

Printed in the United States of America

Contents

Foreword

In Shakespeare's immortal play *Hamlet*, the young Danish aristocrat Horatio has clearly been astonished and disconcerted by his encounter with a ghostlike apparition on the castle battlements. "There are more things in heaven and earth," his friend Hamlet assures him, "than are dreamt of in your philosophy."

Many people today would readily agree with Hamlet that the world and the vast universe surrounding it are teeming with wonders and oddities that remain largely outside the realm of present human knowledge or understanding. How did the universe begin? What caused the dinosaurs to become extinct? Was the lost continent of Atlantis a real place or merely legendary? Does a monstrous creature lurk beneath the surface of Scotland's Loch Ness? These are only a few of the intriguing questions that remain unanswered, despite the many great strides made by science in recent centuries.

Lucent Books' Mystery Library series is dedicated to exploring these and other perplexing, sometimes bizarre, and often disturbing or frightening wonders. Each volume in the series presents the best-known tales, incidents, and evidence surrounding the topic in question. Also included are the opinions and theories of scientists and other experts who have attempted to unravel and solve the ongoing mystery. And supplementing this information is a fulsome list of sources for further reading, providing the reader with the means to pursue the topic further.

The Mystery Library will satisfy every young reader's fascination for the unexplained. As one of history's greatest scientists, physicist Albert Einstein, put it:

> The most beautiful thing we can experience is the mysterious. It is the source of all true art and science. He to whom this emotion is a stranger, who can no longer wonder and stand rapt in awe, is as good as dead: his eyes are closed.

ETs in History and the Imagination

"No one would have believed," wrote the great English novelist H.G. Wells in 1898,

> that this world was being watched keenly and closely by intelligences greater than man's and yet as mortal as his own. . . . No one gave a thought to the older worlds of space as sources of human danger, or thought of them only to dismiss the idea of life upon them as impossible or improbable. . . . Yet across the gulf of space, minds that are to our minds as ours are to those of the beasts that perish, intellects vast and cool and unsympathetic, regarded this Earth with envious eyes, and slowly and surely drew their plans against us.[1]

So begins the first widely read depiction of beings from another world penned in modern times—Wells's *The War of the Worlds*. Now deemed a classic of English literature, during the twentieth century the novel was a major factor in the popularization of the concept that other planets might be inhabited.

Writers coined several words to describe such beings. One is aliens, in reference to their foreign origins. Another, more colloquial one—"little green men"—became popular in the 1950s, when a number of movies stereotyped aliens as short creatures with greenish-colored skin. In more recent decades, the term extraterrestrial has come to be widely accepted by both scientists and the public. The term comes from the words extra, here meaning "beyond," and terrestrial, meaning "relating to Earth"; thus, extraterrestrials (or ETs) are beings "from beyond Earth."

Movie and television shows frequently depict extraterrestrials as "little green men" who use ray guns and other advanced weapons to menace Earth.

Wells's extraterrestrials are Martians, who attempt to invade Earth because the planet Mars is becoming uninhabitable. In the years following the novel's release, few if any people actually worried about a Martian invasion. After all, the story is clearly fictional. Yet the steady rise of industrialization and technology in the twentieth century made the spaceships and advanced weapons used by Wells's Martians seem more believable than they would have been in past eras. Indeed, several recent opinion polls show that a majority of people believe either that extraterrestrial life exists or that there is at least a chance that it does. And this has been directly attributed, in part, to the widespread use of advanced machines and scientific principles and applications. Some aspects of technology have allowed people to begin exploring outer space; and as a result, interest in and curiosity about the universe has become commonplace. Noted philosopher-scientist Paul Davies writes:

> The development of the tools of aerial warfare—especially jet aircraft, radar, rockets and the atomic bomb—sensitized people to the threat from the sky. It seemed but a small step from the reality of the V2 missile [used by Germany against England in World War II] to that of interplanetary spacecraft carrying aliens with superior weaponry. Science-fiction writers, cartoonists and film-makers played on these fears, and the era of space-age fiction, from *Superman* to *Star Wars*, began in earnest. The postwar years also saw a huge rise in the number of reports of unidentified flying objects (UFOs). Many people became convinced that the Earth is being visited regularly by aliens in saucer-shaped spacecraft. With the launch of artificial satellites, and the development of the manned space program culminating in the lunar landings, people came to take space travel for granted. In the popular mind today, there is little difficulty in believing in extraterrestrial beings who regularly ply the galaxy in high-tech spaceships.[2]

Empty Worlds Unthinkable?

Yet the concept of extraterrestrials is far from new, and the possibility of the existence of life beyond Earth has been considered, debated, and sometimes outright accepted since ancient times. In fact, numerous ancient Greek and Roman thinkers and writers advocated the existence of other worlds and alien life. According to the fourth-century B.C. philosopher Metrodorus, for example, "To consider the Earth as the only populated world in infinite space is as absurd as to assert that in an entire field of millet, only one grain will grow."[3] Another Greek thinker of the same period, Epicurus, agreed, writing in a letter to the noted Greek historian Herodotus:

> There is an infinite number of worlds, some like this world, others unlike it. . . . For the atoms out of which a world might arise, or by which a world might be formed, have not all been expended on one world. . . . Nobody can prove that [there could be life] in one sort of world [such as Earth] . . . whereas in another sort of world there could not possibly be the seeds out of which plants and animals arise.[4]

In a like manner, the first-century B.C. Roman philosopher Lucretius, the first-century A.D. Greek biographer Plutarch, the second-century A.D. Greek writer Lucian of Samosata, and many others argued that other inhabited worlds exist. (A notable exception was the fourth-century B.C. Greek thinker Aristotle, who insisted that Earth was the center of all things and the only inhabited world.)

The reasoning behind this wide acceptance of extraterrestrial life in ancient times was that it seemed only natural and logical. The idea that a god or gods would create a world and leave it empty and barren seemed senseless, wasteful, even unthinkable. This argument is here summed up by the late, great science writer Isaac Asimov:

> The world we know—Earth—is full of life, and it is only natural to think that life is as inevitable a characteristic of worlds generally as solidity is. Again, if one thinks of the Earth as having been created by some deity or deities, then it is logical to suppose the other worlds to have been so created as

The Greek philosopher Epicurus advocated a number of forward-thinking scientific concepts, including the existence of atoms and other inhabited worlds.

well. It would then seem nonsensical to suppose that any world would be created and left empty. What motivation could there be in creating empty worlds? What a waste it would be![5]

From Heresy to Scientific Revolution

This view changed markedly, however, after the ancient world declined and Europe entered the Middle Ages (or medieval times). The Roman Catholic Church came to dominate society, and leading churchmen exerted a powerful influence over the way people viewed the universe and humanity's place within it. They firmly rejected the concept of other inhabited worlds because it did not seem to conform to the biblical account of the creation. To support their view, they invoked Aristotle, who by that time was mistakenly seen as an almost infallible sage.

This conception of an uninhabited alien planet would have been unthinkable to most ancient scientists, who viewed an empty world as wasteful.

Those who challenged the church's stance on life beyond Earth paid a heavy price. One was an Italian friar and philosopher named Giordano Bruno, who had the audacity to suggest that the stars are other suns, that infinite planets exist, and that these planets are surely populated by people. In 1600 the church accused Bruno of heresy (going against church doctrines) and burned him at the stake.

Yet the scientific revolution that had begun shortly before Bruno's death was rapidly gaining steam. In the 1500s Polish astronomer Nicolas Copernicus had demonstrated that the Sun, and not Earth, lay at the center of things, and that Mars, Jupiter, and the other planets were worlds like Earth. In this view, the planets were part of the Sun's family—the solar system (from Sol, an ancient name for the Sun). More and more scientists began to accept this notion, including German astronomer Johannes Kepler. In a work titled *Conversation with a Sidereal Messenger*, written in 1610, he states:

Our moon exists for us on Earth, not the other globes. Those four little moons [recently discovered orbiting Jupiter] exist for Jupiter, not for us. Each planet in turn, together with its occupants, is served by its own satellites. From this line of reasoning we deduce with the highest degree of probability that Jupiter is inhabited.[6]

Thanks to Kepler and others like him, it once more became fashionable to discuss the possibility of extraterrestrial life. Many nonscientists did so in the following three centuries, including the brash Englishman-turned-American patriot Thomas Paine (author of the famous 1776 pamphlet *Common Sense*). In his work *The Age of Reason*, he writes:

The inhabitants of each of the worlds of which our [solar] system is composed enjoy the same

An illustration from a book published in 1750 shows the six planets then known and their moons. Many people speculated that these worlds were inhabited.

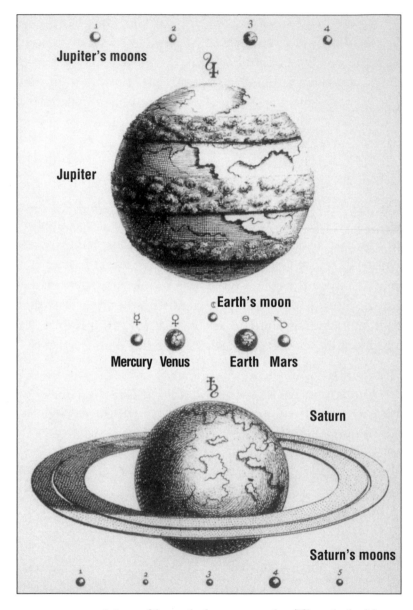

opportunities of knowledge as we do. They behold the revolutionary motions of our Earth, as we behold theirs. All the planets revolve in sight of each other, and, therefore, the same universal school of science presents itself to all. Neither does the knowledge stop here. The system of worlds next to us exhibits, in its revolutions, the same principles and school of science to the inhabitants of their system, as our system does to us, and in like manner throughout the immensity of space.[7]

Many respected scientists also accepted the idea of beings on other planets, including French astronomer Camille Flammarion in his 1862 book *On the Plurality of Habitable Worlds.*

Canals on Mars?

However, although there was a fair amount of interest in and discussion about extraterrestrial life, no one had yet offered any tangible or even circumstantial evidence for it. This situation changed abruptly in 1877 when Italian astronomer Giovanni Schiaparelli claimed to have observed faint lines crisscrossing the surface of Mars. Schiaparelli himself did not advocate that these were artificial constructions. But others did. In 1892, for instance, Flammarion published a book titled *The Planet Mars*, in which he argued that the lines on the red planet might be canals built by intelligent Martians.

The idea excited people of all walks of life, including a wealthy American named Percival Lowell. Convinced that the lines on Mars were canals, he built Lowell Observatory in Flagstaff, Arizona, chiefly to study that planet. Lowell drew detailed maps of the canals and eventually published his own book, *Mars as the Abode of Life.* All of this talk of possible intelligent Martians soon inspired H.G. Wells to write his great novel, in which a drying climate and failing canal system motivate the Martians to seek greener pastures—namely Earth.

Up until the time of Flammarion, Lowell, and Wells, many scientists and nonscientists alike had shared the general belief that life on other planets was a distinct possibility. However, in the early twentieth century the views of most scientists changed. Astronomers increasingly verified that conditions on the other planets in the solar system are hostile to life, at least to Earth-like life. Also, close-up photos taken of Mars showed conclusively that the so-called canals had been optical illusions. So the consensus became that the possibility of extraterrestrial life is unlikely.

Despite these doubts expressed by the scientific establishment, however, the general public in developed countries like the United States and England did not stop believing that alien life might exist. This can be seen in the reactions to entertainer Orson Welles's radio dramatization of H.G. Wells's *The War of the Worlds* in 1938. Welles changed the story's setting from England in the 1890s to New Jersey in the 1930s; and tens of thousands of listeners who tuned in too late to hear the show's traditional introduction and theme music believed an actual invasion was under way.

Many people were equally disturbed and/or intrigued when the first sightings of flying saucers (later called UFOs) began in the late 1940s. Large numbers of people became convinced that not only are extraterrestrials a real possibility, but also they might actually be visiting Earth. And the strength of this growing conviction was reflected in the widespread popularity of a new genre of movies about alien invaders or contact with extraterrestrials. Among the biggest hits were *The Day the Earth Stood Still*, *The Thing*, and the film version of Wells's *The War of the Worlds* in the 1950s; *2001: A Space Odyssey* in the 1960s; *Star Wars* in the 1970s; *E.T.: The Extra-Terrestrial* and *Close Encounters of the Third Kind* in the 1980s; and *Independence Day* in the 1990s.

Searching for ETs

In the meantime, new generations of scientists who grew up with these films, as well as the various *Star Trek* television series and films, came to be more open-minded about the possibility of extraterrestrial life. Although the scientific community remains divided on the subject, enough astronomers and other scientists find the possibility of alien life credible enough to devote time and money to the quest to find it. A number of systematic searches for extraterrestrial signals are presently under way. No one can predict if these efforts will ever be successful, but if they are, the impact on human society will be nothing less than monumental. As Davies puts it:

A New Jersey man waits for invading Martians after hearing Orson Welles's show claim that spaceships had landed in the area.

There is little doubt that even the discovery of a single extraterrestrial microbe [germ], if it could be

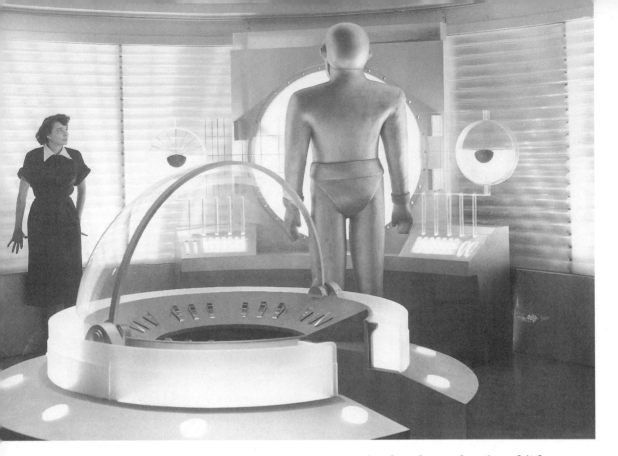

Patricia Neal's character confronts the robot policeman Gort inside an alien spacecraft in the acclaimed 1951 film The Day the Earth Stood Still.

shown to have evolved independently of life on Earth, would drastically alter our world view and change our society as profoundly as the Copernican and Darwinian revolutions. It could truly be described as the greatest scientific discovery of all time. In the more extreme case of the detection of an alien message, the likely effects on mankind would be awesome.[8]

Chapter 1

How Likely or Common Is Extraterrestrial Life?

People have speculated about the existence of life beyond Earth for thousands of years. Even before humans realized that the stars they saw at night are other suns, each of which might have planets like Earth, they wondered if people, animals, and other living things dwelled in the far reaches of the celestial unknown. Today, with the full knowledge that other suns and planets *do* exist, the question "is anyone out there?" remains as compelling as ever. Noted scientist Frank Drake wrote a book with that very title, in which he states:

> Forty years as an astronomer have not quelled my enthusiasm for lying outside after dark, staring up at the stars. It isn't only the beauty of the night sky that thrills me. It's the sense I have that some of those points of light are the home stars of beings not so different from us, daily cares and all, who look across space with wonder, just as we do.[9]

Drake's conjecture about beings who "wonder, just as we do" is a crucial element in defining the nature of possible life beyond Earth. Extraterrestrial life, if it exists, will encompass all manner of plant and animal species. Most of these will likely be nonintelligent, but a few may possibly be as intelligent as human beings. Some scientists are uncomfortable with using the word intelligent to describe such beings, however. Indeed, the word can be misleading because it can be applied in too many general, relative ways. For example, many dog owners brag that their pets are intelligent. And dogs clearly *are* highly intelligent creatures as compared to lower life-forms such as reptiles, fish, and worms.

A more precise term is sentient, which means conscious, self-aware, and able to "wonder," as Drake puts it. Sentient beings will be capable of making tools and constructing a civilization, and, when technologically advanced enough, of traveling into space. For the sake of accuracy and clarity, therefore, it will be preferable to refer to life as either sentient or non-sentient.

The central question for scientists and laypeople alike is not whether sentient beings, along with non-sentient ones, *can* evolve in the universe. After all, the development of life, including the sentient kind, has definitely happened at least once—here on Earth. Instead, people want to know how likely such biological scenarios are. Is life fairly common in the universe, or is it a rare occurrence? And even if more primitive, non-sentient life *is* fairly common, are sentient races as advanced or even more advanced than humans common or rare? At present, no one can answer these questions with any kind of certainty. Yet scientists already have enough clues to make some fascinating and sometimes compelling educated guesses.

The Model of the Early Earth

Most of these clues come from examining the nature of life on Earth. Because the living things on this planet are for the moment the only biological examples scientists can study, they often try to use Earth life as a yardstick, or model, in measuring the conditions needed for life elsewhere. They do not expect that extraterrestrial life, if it exists, will be the same as Earth life. But they do make the general assumption that certain basic chemicals and physical conditions must exist anywhere for life to get started.

The chemicals and conditions that gave rise to life on Earth existed when the planet was in its primordial, or very ancient, form. Earth had only recently accreted, or come together under the force of gravity, from masses of dust, gas, and planetesimals (chunks of metal, rock, and ice) orbiting the young Sun. At first, the planet experienced intense bombardment from planetesimals. After a while, however, as the planet neared its present size, the rain of planetesimals decreased in intensity; yet it was still happening on a lesser scale (as it still does) when the first living things appeared.

Scientists are still somewhat unsure about how these first life-forms developed. But they have attempted to reproduce in the laboratory the conditions on the early Earth in order to see if organic substances can develop from inorganic ones under such conditions. Although organic substances are not themselves alive, they make up the building blocks of living organisms (plants or animals); for example, amino acids are organic chemicals that form the proteins making up the tissues of living things.

The classic experiment relating to the primordial formation of organic substances was conducted in 1953 by Stanley Miller, a graduate student at the University of Chicago, and his professor, Harold Urey. They suspected that the action of lightning, radiation, and other kinds of energy on inorganic chemicals in Earth's early soils and

Bolts of lightning may have caused inorganic chemicals floating in Earth's early seas to change into organic ones.

seas may have sparked the formation of the first living cells. Among the most common inorganic substances on the planet at that time were water, methane, and ammonia. As Paul Davies describes it:

> Miller and Urey introduced water, methane, and ammonia into a glass flask and passed an electric discharge through the mixture for several days. The liquid turned red-brown. On examination, the flask was found to contain several amino acids—organic chemicals found in all living organisms on Earth.[10]

In the years that followed, many scientists repeated and enlarged on Miller's and Urey's work. In all cases, the results were similar—the formation of organic substances in the laboratory. "Although the Miller-Urey experiment was a far cry from the artificial creation of life," Davies points out,

> the experiment gave the impression that if some of the basic building blocks of life could be synthesized [put together] in a few days, then, by leaving the experiment to run for long enough, living organisms might appear. Many scientists came to believe that, given the right conditions and an appropriate soup of chemicals, life would originate spontaneously over a period of millions of years. It followed that if this state of affairs had come about on Earth, it could also have come about on other planets, too.[11]

Did Life's Precursors Come from Space?

At the heart of these experiments lies the assumption that all of the steps leading from nonliving materials to living materials took place on the land and in the seas of the primitive Earth. This trial-and-error process would naturally occur very slowly; so the development of even the simplest one-celled animals could possibly take at least a billion, perhaps even 2 billion or more, years. However, recent discoveries suggest that many of the organic chemicals needed to initiate life developed in space and came to Earth on the planetesimals and other cosmic debris that rained down on the planet in its infancy. Today these objects are called comets and meteors. (Comets are composed of a mixture of ice and rock; meteors are made of metal or rock or both and are called meteorites after they hit the ground). Experts estimate that even today as much as thirty tons (equal in weight to three school buses) of organic materials fall into Earth's atmosphere each day; therefore, many thousands of tons of these materials must have arrived each day when the planet was young.

Scientists have identified these organic substances both in space and on meteorites found on Earth. According to science writer Joe Alper:

> Today, the list of chemicals detected in space ranges from the amino acid glycine up to complex [molecules] similar to those found in coal or heavy petroleum. . . . In addition, researchers have isolated a wealth of organic compounds from meteorites, particularly the 4.6 billion-year-old Murchison meteorite, which fell in Australia in 1969, and the . . . Orgueil meteorite that struck France in 1864. The compounds obtained from meteorites include almost all of the amino acids found in earthly life, as well as many more that aren't found in Earth's biosphere. They also contain nucleic acids (the building blocks of our genes) and . . . a great variety of [other] organics vital to biochemical reactions.[12]

The arrival on Earth of these precursor chemicals of life may well explain why the fossil record shows that the development of primitive living cells on the planet occurred relatively rapidly. Earth formed roughly 4.5 billion years ago; and primitive life appeared no later than .7 billion years later. "The jump from organic chemicals to life is huge," says NASA scientist Scott Sandford, "but if molecules from space had something to do with the development of life here, then that means they're always available to help with the development of life wherever suitable conditions exist in the universe."[13]

Possible Martian Life

Surely such suitable conditions for life have arisen many times among the large numbers of star systems (other solar systems) and planets in the vast reaches of the universe. Yet before considering the possibilities of life in other star sys-

A scientist examines a piece of a meteorite for evidence of primitive life-forms. One Martian meteorite seems to contain such evidence.

tems, it makes sense to examine the situation closer to home first. It is certainly possible that some kind of life, even if very primitive, may have developed in other parts of the solar system.

Among the planets and other bodies making up the solar system, Mars has long been a popular candidate for life, in reality as well as in fiction. "There are good reasons to think that life may have emerged on Mars about the same time it began on Earth," say science writers Terence Dickinson and Adolf Schaller.

Between three and four billion years ago, Martian volcanoes probably spewed enough water vapor over the planet to create an ocean more than 30 meters [98 feet] deep. That's when the riverbeds [visible on the planet] must have been carved out. Now, though, what water is left is frozen in the polar caps and as permafrost beneath the surface. Did life forms develop before all the water froze? Until Mars is explored more thoroughly, we will have to wait for the answer to that question. But if future explorers do discover evidence of past life on Mars, it will tell us that life as we know it is not limited to the surface of Earth.[14]

Oddly enough, humans may not have to travel all the way to Mars to find evidence that life once existed (and still may exist) on that planet. About 16 million years ago, a large asteroid or comet collided with Mars and blasted some Martian rocks into space. After wandering the solar system, roughly thirteen thousand years ago one of these rocks was attracted by Earth's gravity and landed in Antarctica, where human explorers found it in 1984. (They knew it came from Mars because traces of gases trapped inside the object exactly match the Martian atmosphere, which was precisely measured by an Earth probe that landed on Mars in 1976.)

The meteorite, dubbed ALH 84001, has been intensively studied. And imbedded in it scientists have found fossilized (stone-like) microscopic shapes that strongly resemble living and fossil Earth bacteria. The scientific community is still undecided over whether these tiny Martian artifacts are the remains of life or just mineral grains that look like it. But more sophisticated tests performed on them in 2002 suggest that at least some of these are true fossils of extraterrestrial bacteria.

Life in Subsurface Seas?

Also promising as an abode of primitive life in the solar system is Europa, one of the four largest moons of Jupiter.

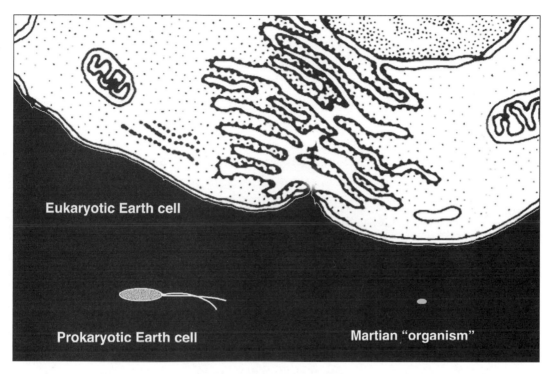

Eukaryotic Earth cell

Prokaryotic Earth cell

Martian "organism"

NASA's Galileo spacecraft, which began orbiting Jupiter in 1995, has provided strong evidence for the existence of a liquid ocean beneath Europa's icy outer shell. This means that water, one of the three main conditions for life, is present in abundance. (The other two conditions are a source of energy and a supply of organic compounds.) Science writer Dana Mackenzie elaborates:

This illustration compares the sizes of some typical Earth microbes with the tiny fossil-like shapes found in the Martian meteorite ALH 84001.

> At first, scientists believed the ice [covering Europa] was up to 100 miles thick. But some planetary scientists argue that . . . the ice may be as thin as one mile, and it may have been breached with slushy geysers [vertical water fountains like Old Faithful in Yellowstone National Park] or shaken by daily "Europaquakes." Once thought to be devoid of sunlight or other sources of energy, Europa may have warm spots under its ice that support periodic "blooms" of microscopic life.[15]

If Europa's ice is thin enough, these "warm" spots might be produced by an energy source such as sunlight or heavy doses of radiation from Jupiter. However, life might also have formed thanks to another energy source, geothermal heat—that is, heat radiating up from Europa's warm core. Such life might be similar to several strange organisms recently discovered living around geothermal vents at the bottoms of Earth's oceans. Among these are one-celled creatures known as lithoautotrophic microbes. According to Gerald A. Soffen of NASA's Goddard Space Flight Center:

> These "bugs," as microbiologists like to call bacteria, live at the bottom of the ocean . . . and obtain their energy from hydrogen, methane, and hydrogen sulfide produced by geochemical reactions of undersea volcanic activity. Their nutrient carbon and nitrogen sources come from dissolved substances in the ocean. Geologists and microbiolo-

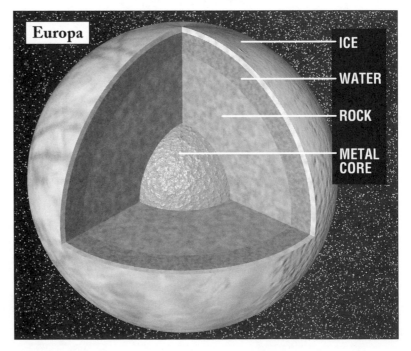

Europa

ICE
WATER
ROCK
METAL CORE

A computer-generated image shows what Jupiter's moon Europa may look like inside. The sea located beneath the icy surface may contain living things.

gists joined forces to explore subsurface environments, examining core samples from a kilometer below the surface. There they have found a whole population of lithoautotrophs, which apparently had remained completely isolated from the surface for millions of years. Does this open the door for subsurface ecologies on other worlds? One thing to remember is that many of these vent-dwellers do not require sunlight. Their energy is derived from chemical reactions. . . . This has profound implications for life on places such as [Jupiter's] moon Europa, where the surface is covered with ice but the interior may be warm enough to allow life-sustaining liquid water.[16]

Earth's history has shown that where single-celled creatures arise, multicelled ones are likely to develop, too. The possibility of such increasingly complex life-forms developing deep in Europa's oceans inspired science-fiction writer Arthur C. Clarke in his great novel *2010: Odyssey Two*. In the story, a race of super-intelligent and very powerful extraterrestrials detects primitive creatures struggling to survive beneath Europa's surface. The super ETs put the Europans on the road to sentience by stimulating the development of their mental abilities; and to make sure that humans do not interfere, Earth craft are forbidden to approach or land on Europa. Real Earth scientists would certainly be upset if they were somehow restricted from exploring Europa. As Mackenzie says, "Depending on whom you talk to, Europa has become our best or second-best hope for finding extraterrestrial life in our solar system."[17]

Meanwhile, oceans of liquid water may also lie beneath the icy shells of Ganymede, another of Jupiter's moons, and Triton, Neptune's largest satellite. The subsurface sea on Ganymede (which at 3,270 miles across is the largest

NASA's Galileo spacecraft passes Ganymede (at left), Jupiter's largest moon. Ganymede may have a subsurface water ocean like Europa's.

moon in the solar system) was also confirmed by the Galileo probe. Ganymede's ocean may be three miles deep, making the volume of water on the moon nearly as large as that on Earth. "If we find that life exists on Europa," says Galileo mission scientist Krishan Khurana, "I would be surprised if it doesn't exist on Ganymede. There are similar conditions on both worlds."[18]

Untold Billions of Stars and Planets

The reason that the oceans on Europa, Ganymede, and/or Triton lie beneath deep layers of ice is that it is simply too cold in the outer planetary region for liquid water to exist on the surface of a planet or moon. (It is also doubtful that high intelligence and a technological civilization could develop in an underwater ocean completely isolated from the rest of the universe; so any life-forms that might exist in these seas are likely relatively primitive.) These moons are therefore said to lie outside of the solar system's "habitable zone," the relatively warm region where liquid water *can* exist on planetary surfaces. (The inner edge of a star system's habitable zone is the point where heat from the star will begin boiling away the liquid water; and the outer edge is the point where the water will start to freeze over.)

Stable Stars Needed for Life?

In this excerpt from their acclaimed book *Intelligent Life in the Universe*, astronomers Carl Sagan and I.S. Shklovskii make the point that the rise of life on a planet may be influenced by the stability of the heat and radiation emitted by its parent star.

For a star to have a habitable planetary system, the radiation emitted by it must remain approximately constant for perhaps billions of years. Other factors being equal, a few percent change in the solar luminosity would have drastic effects on the temperature of the Earth. The overwhelming majority of stars . . . are remarkably constant in their radiation output. Geo-

logical studies indicate that our own Sun has varied its luminosity no more than a few tenths of one percent over the last few hundreds of millions of years. There is, however, a large class of variable stars where luminosities fluctuate greatly. Such stars are unlikely to have habitable planetary systems.

Earth supports life partly because the Sun is a stable star.

As the real possibility of life on Europa shows, not all life must exist in a star's habitable zone. But most scientists believe that a majority of alien life-forms, especially those that build complex civilizations, will originate in stellar habitable zones.

This talk of planets and habitable zones in other star systems presupposes that such planets and systems do exist. Yet before 1995, no one knew for sure if other stars had planets, although both astronomers and laypeople had long considered it highly likely. In October of that year, two Swiss astronomers, Michael Meyor and Didier Queloz, discovered the first extrasolar planet (i.e., one located beyond the solar system).[19] They named it 51 Pegasi (after Pegasus, the flying horse, the constellation in which they found it). The planet lies very close to its parent star, so it is too hot (at least twenty-five hundred degrees Fahrenheit) to support life.

Still, the discovery of 51 Pegasi proved at last that the planets orbiting our Sun are not unique. In the months and years that followed, many more extrasolar planets were found. Among the newest, discovered in the summer of 2003, is one that orbits HD70642, a faint star in the constellation Puppis. The planet lies at a distance of ninety light-years from Earth. (A light-year is the distance light travels in a year, or about 6 trillion miles.) It is about the size of Jupiter and moves around its star in a circular orbit, similar to Jupiter's in our own solar system. This suggests to astronomers that smaller, rocky planets like Earth and Mars may lie closer to the star, also as in our solar system. The discovery of this Jupiter-like body brought the number of known extrasolar planets to 110.

Such bodies continue to be found in increasing numbers, all orbiting stars relatively near the Sun. The fact that numerous stars in a single small area of space have planets suggests that a hefty percentage of stars in other areas will also have them; so planets must be common, not rare, throughout the universe. Even in a worst-case scenario, in which less than 10 percent of stars have planets and those that do have only two or three, the number of planets is enormous. Consider that there are at least 100 billion stars in the Milky Way galaxy alone. (A galaxy is a huge collection of stars held together by their combined gravities; the local galaxy, in which the Sun and its family reside, is called the Milky Way.) A neighboring galaxy, Andromeda, may have 200 billion or more stars. And untold billions of other galaxies exist, stretching all the way to the farthest limits that human telescopes can see.

How Many Sentient Races?

Given this staggering immensity of stars and planets and the abundance of organic materials in space, many scientists feel that it is unlikely that life arose only once in the whole universe. Primitive and/or more advanced forms of non-sentient life may exist on thousands, perhaps even millions, of planets in each galaxy. If so, some experts contend, extraterrestrial sentient life, even if somewhat rare, is likely to exist, too. Not all of these ETs, if they *are* out there, will be capable of communicating with humans and other distant races. After all, the ancient Egyptians were sentient beings, but they lacked the knowledge and technology to contact alien planets.

To help scientists estimate the possible number of sentient civilizations capable of such communication, in 1961 Frank Drake devised a mathematical equation that has come to be known, appropriately, as the Drake equation. Later refined by astronomers Carl Sagan and Joseph Shklovskii, the equation factors in the following variables: the number of stars in the Milky Way; the estimated fraction of these stars that have planets; the number of planets in each star system having the conditions needed for life;

the fraction of these planets on which living creatures actually develop; the fraction of these creatures that evolve into sentient beings; the fraction of these sentient races that develop a technological civilization; and the average lifetime of such a civilization.

Obviously, the number of advanced civilizations determined by the equation will vary considerably, depending on how liberal or conservative one is in estimating the various factors involved. For example, if one believes that very few non-sentient life-forms will ever develop into sentient ones, the number of advanced civilizations will be small; and vice versa. Even by extremely conservative estimates, however, many advanced sentient races may exist. Basing their opinion on the equation and several other factors, Sagan and Shklovskii assert:

> The number of extant [existing] civilizations substantially in advance of our own in the galaxy today appears to be perhaps between 50 thousand and one million. The average distance between technical civilizations is between a few hundred light-years and about 1000 light-years. The average age of a communicating technical civilization is 10,000 years or more.[20]

However, other experts disagree with this scenario, saying that it is far too optimistic. Some argue that other sentient races may exist, but they are very rare, perhaps fewer than five or ten in each galaxy, with some galaxies having none at all. Other, even more conservative experts say that humanity is unique—probably the only sentient race in the universe. One common argument invoked to support this view is the "anthropic principle," advanced by physicist Brandon Carter. In this view, the rise of the human race was the result of a set of highly unusual and rare physical circumstances occurring simultaneously, each of which was essential to human development. "The essence of Carter's argument," Paul Davies explains, "is the premise that the formation of intelligent life is an exceedingly improbable event, so improbable, in fact, that its probability is much less than 1."[21] Thus, the evolution of sentient beings on Earth beat the odds in an extreme long shot, and the chances of other living things beating those odds are nearly zero.

Other arguments that no sentient extraterrestrials exist have also been made. Yet it is important to emphasize that most of these ideas were initially advanced well before the confirmation of numerous extrasolar planets and the discovery that many of the organic chemicals needed for life are abundant in space. These and other factors have significantly strengthened the arguments in favor of extraterrestrial life, at least on a primitive level. And a number of biologists advocate that, given enough time and the proper conditions, some primitive organisms will invariably evolve toward higher intelligence. Therefore, Soffen says, "there

Optimistic scientific estimates for the number of sentient civilizations in the universe are based on the number of stars, which is truly vast.

exists a great deal of circumstantial evidence that our search for life elsewhere will not go unrewarded."[22] Noted scientist Clifford Pickover agrees. "Someday in the not-too-distant future," he speculates,

> we will find life on other worlds. The fact that life emerged on Earth suggests that it exists in other parts of the cosmos because the elements of which the entire universe is composed are remarkably uniform. If some of the elements have combined in ways that produce life on Earth, it is likely they have combined in similar ways elsewhere. We have every reason to believe that there are other water-rich worlds in the universe with complex organic molecules. This means that there should be many worlds in the Milky Way capable of supporting simple life-forms. Even as you read these words, there must be planets in other galaxies on which life is just emerging or even flourishing. Just as you blink, some new life-form is arising.[23]

Chapter 2

What Physical Forms Might Extraterrestrials Have?

Nearly everyone has seen some of the make-believe ETs created for movies and television. Some, like Klaatu in *The Day the Earth Stood Still* and Luke Skywalker and his companions in the *Star Wars* films, are completely human-looking. Others are humanoid. That is, they have roughly human shape—a head, a torso, two arms, and two legs—but have certain superficial differences; for instance, they might have different colored skin, snakelike eyes, or high, bony fore-heads, or they might be very short or very tall. Among the examples in this category are the Vulcans (including Mr. Spock) and Klingons in the *Star Trek* universe and E.T. in *E.T.: The Extra-Terrestrial*. Finally, there are the nonhu-manoid film aliens, which range from sluglike (Jabba the Hutt in *Return of the Jedi*) to insectlike (the creatures in *Starship Troopers*) to completely formless (the monster in *The Blob*).

Such beings are certainly entertaining. But are they believable from a scientific standpoint? First, most of the human and humanoid movie ETs are shaped that way either to make it easier for audiences to relate to the aliens or to make it possible for human actors to portray these beings. And most of the nonhumanoid film aliens are purposely designed to look menacing, disgusting, or humorous. "But have you ever wondered whether these aliens actually make sense?" ask science writers Terence Dickinson and Adolf Schaller. "What do they eat? What is their home planet like? What type of air do they breathe?"[24]

Most filmmakers have not seriously addressed these questions. But fortunately a number of scientists and well-informed science-fiction writers have. And they contend that extraterrestrial life will usually differ in form considerably from Earth life, depending on the degree to which the conditions on other worlds differ. As chemist Robert Shapiro and physicist Gerald Feinberg put it:

Warrant Officer Ripley (Sigourney Weaver) gets up close and personal with a menacing extraterrestrial in the first film of the Alien *series.*

The course of organic synthesis [creation of life] in the universe may on some occasions turn in the direction of the chemicals of Earth life, but it is

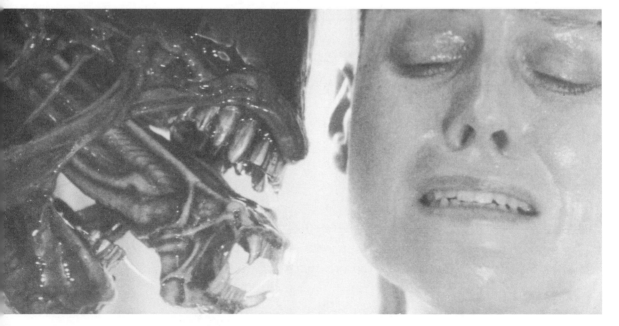

clear that it can take other directions as well. . . . It can take place in a wide variety of environments very different from Earth.[25]

Moreover, even if life on another planet *has* developed under Earth-like conditions, it does not follow that the creatures that evolve there will closely resemble Earth creatures. Billions of species have evolved on Earth since life began on the planet, ranging from one-celled animals to sponges, worms, squids, insects, snakes, whales, birds, bats, dogs, chimps, and people. Yet biologists point out that this bewildering variety of physical shapes has barely scratched the surface of the billions of trillions that are possible on Earth. And keep in mind that all of these are, on the genetic level, related and similar, the results of a single biology that developed under a specific set of conditions on one planet. When one factors in the different conditions and biologies that can exist on millions or billions of alien planets, the number, diversity, and shapes of possible species becomes mind-boggling. In the words of one expert:

> Aliens will not resemble anything we have seen. Considering that octopi, sea cucumbers, and oak trees are all very closely related to us, an alien visitor would look less like us than does a squid. Some fossils [found on Earth] are so alien we can't determine which end of the creatures is up, and yet these monsters evolved right here on Earth from the same origins as we did.[26]

Reproduction, Size, and Symmetry

To some degree, the diversity of physical forms taken by living things on a planet will depend on the complexity of these organisms. The simpler life-forms are the least diverse. So most primitive living things on other worlds will likely resemble those that developed on the young

Earth, namely one-celled organisms. Thus, although some differences will exist, extraterrestrial bacteria will probably not look very different from Earth bacteria. However, as organisms become more and more complex, their chances for diversity increase sharply.

Before considering the wide range of possible physical forms and abilities for alien life, it is important to examine certain general characteristics that all (or at least the vast majority of) living things will have in common. All will ingest (eat) and digest nutrients and then excrete (expel) the waste materials, for example. And all must have the ability to reproduce, or propagate, the species. These are some of the key factors that differentiate living things from nonliving things.

Regarding reproduction, aliens need not, and likely *will* not, necessarily create their young in the same manner as humans and other mammals. This can be seen in the wide variety of ways that other animals and plants reproduce on Earth. Some grow their young inside their bodies, as mammals do, but others lay eggs. Others divide in half, creating two creatures out of one, and still others grow buds that detach and become new members of the species. Alien species may use any and all of these reproductive strategies. Also, some of them may not be limited to two sexual partners, as humans are. A species having three or more genders, all of which play key roles in the reproductive process, is perfectly credible.

Nearly all extraterrestrials, no matter what they look like, will also fit within a certain size range. For example, primitive life-forms have to be at least big enough to incorporate the minimum number of molecules needed to support ingestion, digestion, and reproduction. (A possible minimum size for one-celled creatures may be about 10-millionths of an inch.) Size is just as crucial to more complex life-forms. Creatures with high intelligence, like mammals, cannot be microscopic, nor even as small as ants,

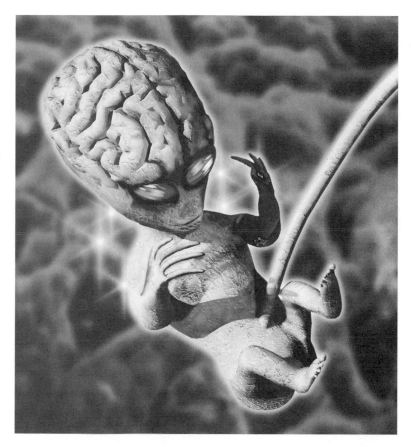

This imaginary alien fetus is attached to its parent by an umbilical cord. If extraterrestrials exist, they likely reproduce in diverse and perhaps strange ways.

because their bodies have to be large enough to support complex circulatory and nervous systems and large brains.

Similarly, there is an *upper* limit to the practical size of a creature. Bones, tendons, and muscles, no matter how strong, can only support so much weight, at least on land. (Sea creatures can be bigger because the water supports much of their weight.) Animals slightly larger than the largest dinosaurs—weighing perhaps one hundred tons— are possible. But a being the size of the fictional Godzilla would simply collapse and suffocate under its own bulk.

A majority of extraterrestrials may also be bilaterally symmetrical, as most Earth animals are. This means that the limbs, eyes, ears, and other body parts on the left side of an imaginary line drawn down the middle of a creature will look the same as those on the right side. Humans have bilateral symmetry, as do other mammals, birds, reptiles, amphibians, fish, and insects. "It appears that our ancestors were aquatic animals," Clifford Pickover writes.

If aliens also evolved from aquatic species, they too may have bilateral symmetry because this is an efficient way to produce a streamlined, muscular body for catching food and fleeing from predators in the water—especially when compared to slower life forms with *radial symmetry* [irregular or uneven form], like the more sedentary [slow or unmoving] starfish, urchins, and jellyfish.[27]

What If the Dinosaurs Had Lived?

It is possible that many sentient aliens might have humanoid shape and upright posture. Indeed, some evidence suggests that right here on Earth other kinds of creatures besides humans could have done so had the impact of a large comet or asteroid not wiped out the dinosaurs 65 million years ago. In 1982 Canadian scientist Dale A. Russell addressed the question of what might have happened if the dinosaurs had survived and mammals had not replaced them as the planet's dominant life-forms. Russell concluded that some dinosaurs might eventually have evolved intelligence comparable to that of humans. He pointed out that some small carnivores, among them the three-foot-tall *Stenonychosaurus*, had unusually large brains for reptiles and were undoubtedly clever pack hunters. The *Stenonychosaurus*'s three-fingered hand also had an opposable thumb, like apes and humans do. This gave it the potential for developing the ability to use tools and thereby of one day constructing a technical civilization. With

the assistance of taxidermist Ron Séguin, Russell constructed a life-size model of the creature's possible intelligent descendant. Russell called it a "dinosauroid." The men based the creature's physical characteristics on logical scientific assumptions. For instance, because the evolving dinosaur's long, skinny neck could no longer support its steadily enlarging brain and skull, the neck shortened and the head moved over the shoulders for extra support. This gave the dinosauroid bipedal posture like that of humans. And because the tail was no longer necessary to counterbalance a long neck, the tail slowly disappeared. The dinosauroid model is on display at the National Museum of Natural Sciences in Ottawa, Canada. It remains a thought-provoking reminder that the course of evolution is subject to many random events. Had it not been for a chance meeting between Earth and a wandering chunk of extraterrestrial matter 65 million years ago, modern civilization might have been built by three-fingered hands.

Although creatures with radial symmetry are likely the less common of the two forms, this does not preclude them from evolving high intelligence, perhaps even sentience. Noted writer Hal Clement quite believably describes such a creature in his novel *Cycle of Fire*. Called an Abyormenite, it has an oblong central trunk from which six tentacles extend. The Abyormenites reproduce by depositing spores in the bodies of other creatures.

Sensory Organs and Abilities

Other physical features that all living things, including alien ones, must have are sensory organs and abilities. These are the means to detect and observe the natural world around them, including locating food and dangerous predators. Common examples on Earth include eyes for seeing, ears for hearing, noses for smelling, and nerves in the skin for touching. Additional sensory methods have been identified on our planet. Both bats and dolphins use a kind of sonar, for instance, in which they send out high-pitched sounds; the sound waves strike various objects and bounce back, revealing the position of and other data about the objects. Also, some fish can sense the presence of other creatures by detecting electrical or magnetic fields. Regarding the latter, Dickinson and Schaller write:

> Earth's magnetic field causes a compass to point to the magnetic poles. In the same way, animals that can sense the magnetic field can use it to determine direction. Some insects, fish and birds have sensors in their brains that use the Earth's magnetic field for navigation and orientation, particularly during periods of migration. If an Earth-like planet were to have a stronger magnetic field than the Earth's, magnetic-field detectors would probably be a more prevalent sensory system in that planet's life forms than on Earth, because it would be easier to sense.[28]

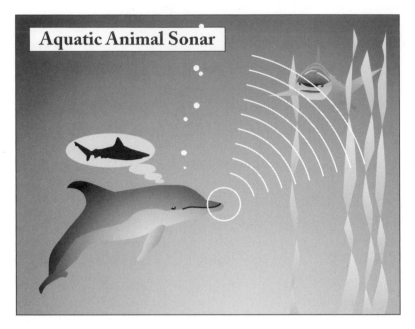

Aquatic Animal Sonar

Thus, many of the same sensory organs and abilities prevalent on Earth will likely exist on alien planets that support life. Eyes of some kind will surely be common. And two eyes will probably be more common than one or three since one provides no depth perception and three task the brain with extra, needless image processing. Even assuming that many or most extraterrestrial creatures do have eyes, however, it does not necessarily follow that they see in the same manner that people do. For one thing, humans see only in visible light, which makes up only a small part of the larger electromagnetic spectrum. It is perfectly feasible that some creatures may see in other parts of the spectrum, such as ultraviolet.

Similarly, some creatures may see things by the amount of thermal radiation, or heat, they give off. Several animals on Earth have some degree of this ability; a mosquito, for example, can detect temperature differences as little as $1/500$ of a degree Celsius. Imagine, then, a race of alien beings whose visual world is shaped by temperature differences. "Consider the analogy of a painting," says Pickover.

When we see a painting we see many different hues not seen by a color-blind animal. (Incidentally, many mammals are color-blind.) Just as we see reds, greens, blues, and all the shades in between, aliens on dark worlds may "see" the world with distinct temperatures. An alien with this ability would perceive and give labels to 100, 101, and 102 degrees in the same way we perceive different colors and name them red, purple, and maroon. . . . Their traffic lights might be hot, warm, and cold instead of red, yellow, and green.[29]

It should be pointed out that not all parts of the spectrum are necessarily useful for ordinary sense perception. An example is radio waves, as explained by Carl Sagan and Joseph Shklovskii:

There is a primary difficulty in imagining organisms which "see" with radio waves. In order to have any useful resolution—that is, detection of fine visual detail—the effective collecting area must be enormous. To have the same resolving power . . . that the [human] eye has . . . an extraterrestrial [radio wave] "eyeball" would have to be roughly half a mile in diameter.[30]

Obviously, such giant eyes would be so awkward and impractical that the chances of them evolving in nature are almost nil.

Another crucial element to sense perception is time. Humans see and otherwise sense the world around them in a certain time frame, which they take for granted is a part of a fixed, unchangeable objective reality. Yet this so-called reality is in many ways an illusion based on the particular manner and speed with which people's brains process incoming information. Pickover briefly explores other possible time frames and perceived realities:

Imagine aliens who could make gestures so quickly that we couldn't see them, but the aliens would have no trouble seeing them. Imagine what it would be like for us to see the vibration of a fly's wing in flight or the intricate array of droplets splashed when a raindrop hits a puddle. If we were able to extend our current senses in range and intensity, we could glimpse alien sense domains. For example, if we possessed sharper sight we would see things that are too small, too fast, too dim, or too transparent for us to see now. We can get an inkling of such perceptions using special cameras, computer-enhanced images, night-vision goggles, [and] slow-motion photography . . . but if we had grown up from birth with these visual skills,

An artist's view of a humanoid extraterrestrial with two eyes. Having two eyes may be common, since having only one provides no depth perception.

our species would be transformed into something quite unusual. Our art would change, our perception of human beauty would change, our ability to diagnose diseases would change, and even our religions would change.[31]

How Do Beings Become Sentient?

The physical elements examined so far—reproduction, size, symmetry, and sensory abilities—are likely characteristic of all (or nearly all) creatures in the universe, both primitive and advanced. Of these creatures, the most compelling for scientists and laypeople alike are the more intelligent beings, especially the sentient ones. Before exploring the possible physical traits of sentient extraterrestrials, however, it is important to consider how they became sentient in the first place.

Many scientists believe that the tendency for higher and higher levels of intelligence to develop is not simply a matter of random chance. Rather, it seems to be built right into the evolutionary system. "Intelligence seems to be a powerful tool for self-preservation," Dickinson and Schaller argue.

> In any particular species, the smart guys get food, while the stupid ones die off. This appears to be a fundamental rule of nature on Earth, and it results in larger and larger brains as life evolves over broad spans of time. If we discover life on another planet, we might also expect to find that the most successful creatures on that alien world are those with the largest brains and the greatest ability to think their way out of trouble and into the next meal. (Of course, if they are advanced beyond us, they may be using their reasoning powers for pursuits we can scarcely imagine.)[32]

This does not mean that all planets where life takes root will end up with sentient beings. But it does suggest that

The large skull of the familiar character E.T., from Steven Spielberg's classic film, indicates that the creature has the big brain necessary for high intelligence.

on most such planets evolution will not remain static; sooner or later, primitive life-forms will give rise to ones that are more complex, both physically and mentally.

Under these conditions, therefore, it is plausible that sentient beings at least occasionally evolve on other worlds. If so, it is logical to wonder whether they will be sentient in the same way humans are; that is, will they view the universe and make use of their intelligence the same way we do? According to scientist Seth Shostak:

> The question is whether intelligence of the sort that can understand and make use of science has evolved elsewhere. How often will nature produce creatures with the characteristics that set us apart from "mere animals"—consciousness, cognition [self-awareness], and creativity? The answer . . . may be "often." Intelligence has sprung up on our planet in response to competitive pressure. When the first humans clambered out of the African savannas, they confronted an environment in which the number of species had reached an all-time high; twice as many as when the dinosaurs held sway. The world was a brutally competitive place. Brain power, like keen eyesight or sensitive hearing, conferred an advantage in this heightened battle for survival. Intelligence promotes adaptability. It may be a common solution to the challenges of a tough, terrestrial environment populated by sophisticated competitors. If life on other planets has similarly become diverse and competitive, it may also produce intelligent creatures.[33]

One thing seems certain. If sentient extraterrestrials do exist, some are likely to have older and more advanced civilizations than the one on Earth. And considering the vast distances that separate stars and the high level of technology that will be needed to cover these distances, any race

capable of interstellar travel will be much more advanced than humanity.

Humanoids and Carbon Compounds

What physical shape will such sentient beings have? To begin with, exact replicas of human beings, as portrayed so often in science-fiction movies, can be immediately ruled out. The human body is the result of billions of biological events and steps, most of them random. These occurred over the course of many millions of years in a peculiar set of environmental conditions existing on Earth. It is extremely unlikely, if not impossible, that all of these events and steps will be repeated in the same order under the exact same environmental conditions on another planet.

That does not rule out the more general humanoid form for some extraterrestrials, however. As Dickinson and Schaller point out:

> For land-dwelling creatures with large brains, the humanoid form has many advantages. For one thing, it frees the upper limbs—the hands—to make tools and develop technology. Also, if the

head is anywhere but on the short neck directly atop the body, the bone structure and muscles required to support it are more massive and therefore less versatile than the humanoid's. We think it may be reasonable to assume that any land creature which walks on two legs and has a heavy head because of a big brain would be humanoid in form no matter what it initially evolved from.[34]

Assuming that a good many intelligent and sentient aliens do possess humanoid shape, it is important not to confuse humanoids with humans. The famous meat-eating dinosaur *Tyrannosaurus rex* was humanoid (with the addition of a tail), as are many apes; and on screen, E.T. and the monster in the *Alien* films can be classified as humanoid. Yet none of these creatures (with the possible exception of the apes) is even nearly human-looking.

Also, regardless of how many intelligent and sentient ETs may have roughly humanoid form, many others probably do not. And this may be closely related to their chemical makeup. All life on Earth is based on, or structured around, compounds containing carbon and the use of water as a solvent (a medium in which these compounds are suspended or dissolve). Shapiro and Feinberg write:

> Our own chemical system, particularly in its use of water as a solvent, and carbon as the key building block of large molecules, is uniquely fit for the purpose of sustaining life. . . . The special properties of carbon include its ability to bond to itself in long chains and to form bonds to four other atoms at one time. An enormous number of compounds containing carbon can, therefore, exist.[35]

Alternative Chemistries and Extreme Habitats

But is it absolutely necessary that carbon compounds, the basis of life on Earth, be present for any kind of life to exist? A growing number of scientists think it may not be. "It is conceivable," say Shapiro and Feinberg, "that a basis for life could be constructed using an alternative chemistry."[36] The element silicon, for instance, forms long chains and bonds to many other elements, much as carbon does (although silicon is not quite as versatile as carbon in this respect). On Earth, silicon is a major ingredient of rocks, sand, and glass. But it might be possible in certain alien environments for silicon compounds to produce organic chemicals using a liquid other than water as a solvent. Liquid ammonia is a possibility.

Some scientists and science-fiction writers have envisioned hypothetical silicon-based beings. Dickinson and Schaller describe a "lithovore," a creature like a giant insect, only made of crystals; it eats rocks and digests them with

Wise old Yoda, from the Star Wars *films, is an example of a humanoid alien who is not very human looking.*

powerful acids. Similarly, in his novel *Conscience Interplanetary*, Joseph Green describes a Cryer, a silicon-based intelligent plant with a central trunk made of crystals and leaves made of sharp glass. Such creatures are theoretically possible. But silicon-based entities do not necessarily have to be similar to crystals or rocks. Softer tissues and even humanoid shapes might be possible for such beings.

If they exist, silicon-based beings will live in physical conditions and habitats that humans and other Earth creatures would find extreme, probably even lethal. Yet one need not turn to fiction or the imagination to find life thriving in extreme, poisonous environments. Indeed, such situations are known right here on Earth. Scientists have found bacteria that flourish in industrial solvents used to clean machines, for example. And microbes have been found living more than two miles under the ground, in boiling hot springs, and under deep layers of ice. Metal-eating bacteria also exist on Earth, along with anaerobes, microscopic creatures that live without oxygen and actually find it toxic; acidophiles, organisms that thrive in acids so powerful they can dissolve human skin in seconds; and halophiles, microbes that can survive only in brine so salty that it kills fish and other animals almost instantly. Biologists sometimes call such organisms living in extreme conditions "extremophiles."

Since extremophiles are found in abundance on Earth, it requires no great leap of the imagination to picture such creatures living in extreme physical conditions on alien worlds. All of Earth's extremophiles seem to be physically primitive. But that probably reflects the fact that they live in isolated environmental niches and cannot evolve toward more complex forms under normal Earth conditions. For example, the abundant oxygen in the planet's atmosphere would impede the development of more advanced versions of oxygen-hating microbes. In contrast, on a planet *without* oxygen (or with very little), such creatures might have a chance to evolve into higher forms. It is interesting to note that sentient oxygen-haters would see themselves as normal and humans and other Earth creatures as weird. "The term extremophile reflects a bias," Pickover points out. "Aliens living in environmental extremes would think *we* were the extremophiles."[37]

Black Clouds and Beethoven

One thing that both extremophiles and more familiar Earth-like creatures have in common is that they all evolve and live on planets. Must this always be the case? Or is the idea that life can only originate on planets a bias of planet dwellers like ourselves? Remember that space is filled with organic materials, some of which may have contributed to the development of life on Earth. It is at least possible that some of these materials have found nonplanetary pathways to life. If so, the beings that evolve in such situations would exist in places humans would not expect to find life; in fact, such beings might not even appear to *be* alive by earthly definitions.

Some astronomers, physicists, and other scientists have tried to visualize what such exotic beings might be like. One of most famous and intriguing is the entity created by noted astronomer Fred Hoyle for his novel *The Black Cloud.* An interstellar cloud thousands of miles in extent and made up of tiny dust grains, the creature has attained sentience by efficiently organizing the otherwise random electrical charges and magnetic forces within its "body."

Other exotic beings postulated by scientists include those composed of plasma (hot gases) and living inside stars; those made up of various kinds of radiation; and those dwelling on or in super-dense objects such as neutron stars. It is admittedly hard for humans to imagine how such truly alien life-forms would interact, construct civilizations, or view the universe (if they even do these things). But as Pickover perceptively points out:

This human astronaut must have oxygen to live. Alien beings who regard oxygen as poisonous would likely view humans as extremophiles.

When viewed from afar, it is equally hard to imagine that interactions between proteins and nucleic acids could possibly lead to the wondrous . . . complexity of Earthly life—from majestic blue whales and ancient redwoods to curious, creative humans who study the stars. If you were a silicon alien from another star system, and you had a . . . list of our amino acids, could you use it to predict the rise of civilization? Could you have imagined a mossy cavern . . . a retina, a seagull's cry, or the tears of a little girl? Would you have foreseen Beethoven, Einstein, Michelangelo, or Jesus?[38]

Chapter 3

Are Extraterrestrial Spacecraft Visiting Earth?

When some people hear the words aliens or extraterrestrials, they immediately think about flying saucers and UFOs. The term flying saucer was coined in 1947, shortly after a businessman and private pilot named Kenneth Arnold claimed he saw nine shiny disks speeding over the Cascade mountain range in Washington State. Arnold told a newspaper reporter that the objects looked like saucers skipping over water; so in his story the reporter called them "flying saucers," which immediately caught on. The term UFOs, which stands for "unidentified flying objects," was introduced the following year by a magazine journalist.

A flying saucer is supposedly a piloted spacecraft from another world. By definition, a UFO might be such a craft but also might be something else, since it remains unidentified. However, most people have come to use the term UFOs more or less interchangeably with flying saucers, to denote extraterrestrial vehicles visiting Earth.

These alleged visitations take several forms. For several years following the Arnold sighting, people of all walks of life claimed they saw strange objects in the sky, often at night, but sometimes in broad daylight. Later, a number of people said they had been invited to board alien spaceships and travel into space. And later still, others reported being abducted and forced into such ships, where they became guinea pigs in strange experiments. Over the years, thousands of books and articles have been written about these incidents, most of them advocating that extraterrestrials are indeed visiting Earth.

Those that hold this view are frequently surprised, irritated, or both that the vast majority of scientists and

Since the term "flying saucer" was coined in 1947, alien craft have most often been depicted as saucer-shaped with raised domes in the middle.

scientifically literate laypeople do not think aliens are visiting our planet. Typically, the believers interpret the skeptics' attitude as a rejection of the very concept of extraterrestrial life. However, as Isaac Asimov points out:

> To say that intelligent life undoubtedly exists somewhere in the depths of space . . . is *not at all* the same thing as saying that these forms of intelligent life are visiting us in great swarms in spaceships disguised as flying saucers, which are continually being sighted but which never make indisputable contact.[39]

The fact is that a great many scientists do believe that some sort of alien life, perhaps even the sentient kind, probably exists somewhere in the universe. But a number of powerful arguments have convinced them that it is unlikely such beings are presently visiting Earth.

A Lack of Hard Evidence

The first and perhaps most compelling of these arguments is that not a single piece of hard evidence has ever been presented that proves beyond a doubt that extraterrestrials are here. By hard evidence, scientists mean a sample of metal, wood, cloth, flesh, or some other material that can be examined in a laboratory. Modern science is intimately familiar with the molecular and genetic makeup of Earth substances; and a metal alloy or sample of genetic material from a another world could be easily differentiated from earthly versions. If large numbers of alien craft have been visiting Earth for decades, as believers contend, it stands to reason that at least a few would leave behind some kind of hard evidence. It is also telling that, of the thousands of individuals who claim to have been aboard such craft, not one has ever taken the pains to retrieve even a small token artifact to corroborate his or her story.

Believers usually counter this argument by pointing to the large number of visual sightings of flying saucers over the years. In their view, these sightings make up the primary proof of their claims. However, such reports depend too much on the physical and mental reliability, as well as the honesty, of the witnesses. Also, these incidents cannot be reproduced and examined later by experts. So they do not constitute hard evidence. The truth is that some people lie about what they have seen, either to gain notoriety or for other reasons. Also, eyewitnesses often make mistakes, especially in situations in which an incident occurs unexpectedly and very quickly, as is the case in most UFO sightings. Most such witnesses likely honestly think they saw a spaceship. But in reality, they saw something they were not able to identify readily and then jumped to the conclusion that it must have been extraterrestrial in origin. According to Asimov:

> Such reports are usually based on the sighting of something that the sighters cannot explain and that they (or someone else on their behalf) explain as representing an interstellar spaceship—often by saying "But what else can it be?" as though their own ignorance is a decisive factor.[40]

The list of objects and phenomena commonly mistaken for alien craft is huge. One of the more common examples is unconventional human aircraft, especially those, like the F-117 A Stealth bomber, that look very different from ordinary airplanes. High-flying military and weather balloons and artificial satellites are also frequently mistaken for alien craft. In addition, many UFO sightings can be accounted for by uncommon weather conditions and various natural phenomena. These include, among others, strange cloud formations; ball lightning (round or odd-shaped lightning that can remain suspended in the air for several seconds or minutes); sun

Blimps, like the giant Graf Zeppelin (pictured landing), have sometimes been mistaken for alien spacecraft.

dogs (reflections of sunlight on ice crystals in the atmosphere); high-flying flocks of birds; meteors; Venus and other bright planets seen through clouds or haze; and the aurora borealis (or northern lights).

Scientists point out that these and other natural phenomena must be ruled out first before considering the more extreme possibility that the witness has seen an extraterrestrial craft. The scientific method has certain tried and true rules for examining and evaluating evidence. One of the most important is known as Occam's razor (or the principle of parsimony), attributed to a medieval scholar, William of Occam. Essentially it states that one should not turn to an extraordinary explanation for an unknown phenomenon until all ordinary ones have been conclusively eliminated. Robert Sheaffer, a leading skeptical investigator of UFOs, elaborates:

> Occam's razor would have prevented any truly scientific UFO researcher from writing that a fungus

growth in the vicinity of an alleged UFO landing was likely caused by energy emitted from the UFO, unless it could be convincingly demonstrated that such a fungus growth is virtually impossible in ordinary circumstances. When the evidence offered in favor of the reality of UFOs is critically examined according to the dictates of Occam's razor, it is clear that there is little or nothing remaining which merits scientific scrutiny, because there is simply no UFO evidence yet presented that is not readily attributed to prosaic [ordinary, mundane] causes.[41]

The Difficulties of Interstellar Travel

Another strong argument against alien visitations consists of the extreme technological difficulties and long time intervals involved in interstellar travel. Indeed, the distances between star systems, not to mention the distances between galaxies, are so enormous as to be daunting even to the most advanced races. The nearest star (actually a group of three stars orbiting one another), Alpha Centauri, is 4.3 light-years (or 26 trillion miles) from Earth; the Milky Way is some 100,000 light-years across; and the nearest large galaxy, Andromeda, lies 2.2 million light-years away. The following scale model, provided by Seth Shostak, puts such mind-bending, almost incomprehensible distances in perspective:

> Imagine our planetary system to be a village, with the Sun in the middle. In this model, Sol [our Sun] is a glowing sphere the size of a soccer ball. Mercury, Venus, Earth, and Mars, no bigger than small beads, are arrayed on the village's central square. Pluto orbits the town, and is hardly larger than a pinhead. But the nearest other star . . . is a soccer ball four thousand miles away. And that is only the nearest star. The array of soccer balls that

comprise the Milky Way galaxy would, on this scale, stretch to the Sun. At 25 times this distance we would encounter the first of the nearer, large galaxies, with it own immense, flattened fields of soccer balls.[42]

Traversing such immense distances would take a great deal of time, even if an alien spacecraft is moving at a high velocity. Consider that Voyagers 1 and 2, human-built robot craft sent to study Jupiter and Saturn in the 1980s, were traveling at about twenty miles per second. At that speed, a spaceship could go from New York to Los Angeles in less than three minutes. This seems very fast. But the same ship moving at the same speed would require forty thousand years to reach Alpha Centauri and a billion years to make it across the Milky Way.

It is reasonable to argue that advanced extraterrestrials will be capable of building much faster spacecraft than humans can. But there are limits to how fast objects can move. Albert Einstein and other physicists have shown that the speed of light cannot be surpassed and that objects moving at large fractions of that velocity would encounter some debilitating problems. What, then, is the practical upper speed limit for interstellar travel? No one knows for sure. But twenty thousand miles per second, a thousand times faster than the Voyagers and about one-ninth the speed of light, is probably in the ball park. Yet even at that velocity, one incredible by human standards, a trip to Alpha Centauri would still take forty years, and the journey across the Milky Way would take some ten thousand years!

Thus, any aliens visiting Earth would need to invest tremendous amounts of their time in the endeavor. It is certainly conceivable that they might have life spans many times longer than human ones. But if so, even journeys to fairly nearby star systems would still consume most of their lives. So it is highly doubtful that the members of the crew of an alien craft would ever see their home planet again. Their expenditure of energy would also be huge. The total amount of fuel, food, and other supplies needed for voyages lasting hundreds or thousands of years would fill a volume at least hundreds of times larger than the spaceship making the journey.

To solve these problems, perhaps the aliens would hibernate during such voyages. This would require extremely advanced medical knowledge since they would have to keep the various bodily systems healthy and functioning for long periods of time. But any creatures intelligent enough to construct interstellar craft may well possess such knowledge. However, it is difficult to imagine any being willing to sleep away more than 90 percent of its life on the uncertain chance that it might find life in a distant star system. And even if such super-committed beings do exist, it is doubtful they will be inclined to waste any time when they finally reach their destination. As Asimov puts it:

Even traveling at the speed of twenty miles per second, NASA's Voyager 1 would take a billion years to cross our galaxy.

> The energy requirements for interstellar travel are so great that it is inconceivable to me that any creatures piloting their ships across the vast depths of

space would do so only in order to play games with us over a period of decades. If they want to make contact, they would *make* contact; if not, they would save their energy and go elsewhere.[43]

The Space Brothers vs. the Grays

In addition to the difficulties of interstellar travel, scientists and other critics point to major inconsistencies in the nature of the supposed extraterrestrial encounters as well as in the physical forms of the aliens themselves. In the 1940s and 1950s, for example, UFO encounters were of two main kinds. First, many people claimed they saw weird lights or objects in the sky, usually traveling at enormous speeds, although sometimes hovering momentarily over trees or buildings.

The other kind of encounter prevalent during this period was supposed contact made with the visitors. The peo-

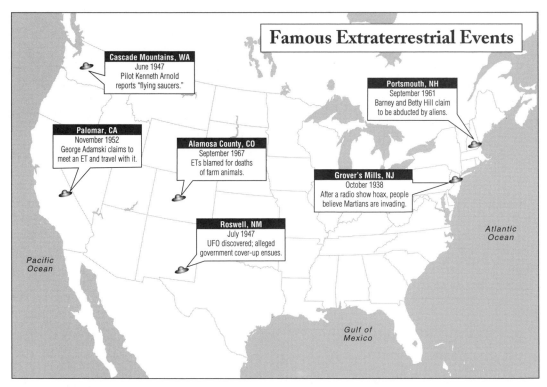

Famous Extraterrestrial Events

Cascade Mountains, WA
June 1947
Pilot Kenneth Arnold reports "flying saucers."

Portsmouth, NH
September 1961
Barney and Betty Hill claim to be abducted by aliens.

Palomar, CA
November 1952
George Adamski claims to meet an ET and travel with it.

Alamosa County, CO
September 1967
ETs blamed for deaths of farm animals.

Grover's Mills, NJ
October 1938
After a radio show hoax, people believe Martians are invading.

Roswell, NM
July 1947
UFO discovered; alleged government cover-up ensues.

Pacific Ocean

Atlantic Ocean

Gulf of Mexico

ple involved, who became known as "contactees," claimed they had conversed with the aliens and in some cases taken rides in their spacecraft. The first and most famous of the contactees was a hamburger cook named George Adamski. He said that in 1952 he met an extraterrestrial in a California desert, a native of the planet Venus named Orthon. According to Adamski, Orthon was concerned that humans had recently developed nuclear weapons, which threatened to contaminate outer space with lethal radiation. Adamski claimed he later voyaged with Orthon and other "space brothers" to the Moon as well as to other planets. All of these aliens were described as tall, unusually handsome humans.

By contrast, the 1960s, 1970s, and 1980s witnessed a rash of alien abduction reports. Typical was the first and most widely publicized case—that of a New Hampshire couple, Betty and Barney Hill. Under hypnosis, they claimed that aliens had forcibly taken them aboard a space-ship and performed experiments on them. Then the beings made them forget, forcing the memories of the unpleasant experience deep into their subconscious. Later abduction stories were similar. The victims usually experienced dreamlike states and loss of memory and endured sexual or other kinds of experimentation by the aliens. The beings in these encounters were almost always described as short, with gray skin, large bald heads, black eyes, and slitlike mouths. (Because of their gray skin, they are often called the "Grays.")

It is instructive to note that the flood of abduction reports did not begin in earnest until after a book about the Hill case appeared in 1966. Similarly, contactees like Adamski did not step forward with their stories until shortly after the release of director Robert Wise's popular 1951 film *The Day the Earth Stood Still*. The movie tells the story of a tall, handsome, human-looking visitor named Klaatu, who comes to Earth because his own people are

Betty and Barney Hill's claim that they were abducted by extraterrestrial beings initiated a wave of similar abduction stories in the 1960s.

worried about human development of nuclear weapons. (After demonstrating his power by neutralizing all electricity and other power around the world, Klaatu warns the natives that they must stop their nuclear experiments or face obliteration.)

The themes and timing of the contactee and abductee phenomena strongly suggest they were inspired by Wise's movie and the book about the Hills, respectively. The tall and noble Klaatu in Wise's film was obviously the model for Orthon and other space brothers described by the contactees; the looks and messages of both were identical and the timing—with the contactee reports directly following the movie's release—was highly suspicious. Similarly, the Hill case almost certainly inspired the initial rash of abduction stories. These then became self-perpetuating, with each new case copying the details of the prior ones. (Not all were fabricated, however. A number of psychologists think that some particularly insecure, fearful people were so moved and disturbed by such stories that they incorporated the images described in them into their own subconscious minds; in this way, they came to believe that they, too, had been abducted and then had their memories repressed.) The point is that the idea that many different kinds of aliens are visiting Earth, all with vastly different physical appearances and contradictory motives, strains credibility.

It is also noteworthy that the number of contactee claims declined sharply after the abduction stories became popular. And in the early 1970s, with the abduction reports at their height, conventional sightings of UFOs like those of the 1940s and 1950s almost ceased entirely. Only one explanation for this rapid decline in contactee stories and saucer sightings seems convincing. Namely, the public largely lost interest in these incidents in favor of abduction tales and stopped manufacturing UFO sightings.

These and other broad differences and inconsistencies in the alien visitations phenomenon suggest that it is based more on changes in social attitudes and popular culture than on real incidents. In that case, the great bulk of UFO sightings and encounters are part of a major modern myth. In science historian Curtis Peebles's view, people created this myth for the same reason they did other myths. Namely, it is a subconscious attempt to create some measure of order and meaning in a world that often seems chaotic and meaningless. "Humans need order," he says,

> which comes both from knowledge and myth. The flying saucer . . . myths are really about how one makes order of his world. The *idea* of disk-shaped alien spaceships becomes the symbol for hopes and

fears about the world. We watch the skies seeking meaning. In the end, what we find is ourselves.[44]

Assessing Alien Motives

Even assuming that the myth hypothesis is wrong and several alien races with different motives are indeed visiting Earth, the motives believers generally give for these visitations are problematic. First, there is the question of their interest in Earth and humans. These beings have supposedly been eavesdropping on the planet for more than half a century, all the while avoiding contact with governments and other authorities and kidnapping and experimenting on the locals. This bespeaks an intense, even morbid fascination with humanity.

Yet how credible is it that in a galaxy of 100 billion stars and innumerable planets, many of which may support life, humans are all that special? "It would be as if every vertebrate in North America somehow felt drawn to a particular house in Peoria, Illinois," Shostak quips.

> Are we really that interesting? It's doubtful that we are, but postulating an alien pilgrimage to our planet validates our importance; even more so if these celestial beings bother to abduct us for sexual experiments or give us a joy ride in their saucers. In light of the fact that any real aliens capable of travel from a distant star system would be enormously more advanced than us, this postulated fascination with humans seems questionable. After all, when Charles Darwin landed in the Galapagos Islands, he didn't offer the iguanas rides on his sailing ship, let alone try to impregnate them. The fact that both Hollywood aliens and those that reportedly flit about the stratosphere *do* take an interest in people suggests that they have been invented for our own purposes. Their task is to show that we are

important in a vast and indifferent universe.[45]

Shostak's mention of alien attempts to mate with and otherwise sexually exploit humans is also telling. The idea that such beings must interbreed with humans in order to strengthen their failing genetic stock is often cited as a motive for extraterrestrial visitations. The absurdity of such a plan becomes apparent, however, when one considers that nature does not even allow different Earth species to interbreed with any success. Chimpanzees and humans evolved in the same biology on the same planet and share close to 99 percent of their genes. Yet a person and chimp cannot produce a child together. For this reason, successful interbreeding between beings that evolved in separate biologies on different planets would be simply out of the question. Carl Sagan sums it up this way:

Alien abductions have been portrayed in numerous books, movies, and television programs.

> Sexual love between a human being and an inhabitant of another planet ignores, in the fundamental sense, the biological realities. . . . A viable offspring would not be possible. . . . Such crossings [between humans and aliens] are about as reasonable as the mating of a man and a petunia.[46]

Another frequently cited motive—that extraterrestrials have come to conquer Earth and exploit its resources—has been a repeated theme of science fiction since H.G. Wells published *The War of the Worlds.* One of the more entertaining recent examples was the movie *Independence Day*. The film's premise is that all of the saucer sightings and abductions since 1947 were preliminary operations leading up to a full-scale invasion of Earth in the late 1990s.

But is such a large-scale operation conducted over such long distances believable? As already established, managing to move even a single craft and its crew across the interstellar gulfs would require enormous expenditures of time and energy. Transporting an invasion fleet large enough to conquer Earth would likely require a large percentage of the entire energy output of the alien civilization, a risky gamble to say the least. Also, communication with and return trips to the home world would take hundreds or perhaps thousands of years.

Moreover, the chances that the aliens in question would be able to breathe Earth's air, eat its food, and live with its germs, all without adverse reactions, is slim. (Wells wisely and carefully addressed this issue in his novel; hav-

The novel The War of the Worlds, *by H.G. Wells, seen at work in the 1940s, incorporated the possibility that aliens will find Earth's germs deadly.*

ing brought humanity nearly to its knees, the Martians are vanquished in the end when Earth's germs infect and kill them.) Most likely the visitors would need to build self-contained environments on Earth to survive. In that case, it would save a great deal of time and energy for them to colonize and exploit an uninhabited planet in their own star system or a neighboring one. Considering these factors, the notion of long-distance interstellar invasions seems highly impractical, if not foolish (but still entertaining).

Finally, it might be argued that the aliens have come to Earth for no other reason than to make contact and establish relations with another sentient species. If so, why have they not done so by now? After all, large-scale sightings of UFOs began in the late 1940s. And some believers think that extraterrestrials have been visiting our planet for hundreds or even thousands of years. These purported aliens must be far more technologically advanced than humans, or else they could not have made the trip from another star system. So it is hardly likely that they are afraid of us. Perhaps they find humans too primitive, insignificant, disgusting, or unworthy to warrant contact. In that case, it would make little sense for them to hang around Earth for decades or centuries, wasting valuable time and resources. In fact, if their motive is simply to make contact with humans, coming in person is not the most efficient way. They could accomplish the task far more economically by flashing electromagnetic signals at us or sending robotic probes to the solar system.

A Continuing Debate

Despite these logical arguments against ongoing alien visitations, diehard believers remain unconvinced. Quite often, they argue that the skeptics have not conclusively proved that such visitations are not happening. Most admit that no hard evidence has yet been found, but they argue that such evidence could be forthcoming at any moment.

Aliens at Different Levels of Development

If they exist, some extraterrestrial races will be far older and more developed than others, says astronomer Seth Shostak in this excerpt from his *Sharing the Universe*. So there is no guarantee they would understand one another and get along.

The Galaxy has been around for 10 billion years or more. Presumably, sentient civilizations have emerged during most of that long history. Needless to say, it's extraordinarily unlikely that two random worlds, separated by hundreds or thousands of light-years, will develop in parallel. No two societies will have left the starting gate at the same time. The disparity will be such that there is little chance that aliens from two societies anywhere in the galaxy will be culturally close enough to really "get along." That is something to ponder as you watch the famous cantina scene in *Star Wars*. In this futuristic pub, a politically correct, multi-hued assemblage of extraterrestrials (all conveniently upright in posture, if not demeanor) share a brew and engage in some back-slapping camaraderie in the grungy port city of Mos Eisely. Does this make sense, given the overwhelmingly likely situation that galactic civilizations differ in their level of evolutionary development by thousands or millions of years? Would you share drinks with a trilobite [a primitive marine creature], an orangutan, or a saber-toothed tiger? Or would you just arrange to have a few specimens stuffed and carted off to the local museum?

Believers also say that Einstein might have been mistaken, and that the speed of light is not the fastest velocity possible. If so, they argue, it is perfectly feasible that beings with advanced technology could reach Earth from anywhere in the galaxy in a relatively short amount of time; thus, scientists and believers are bound to continue disagreeing on the subject of alien visitation for some time to come.

Chapter 4

The Ongoing Search for Sentient Extraterrestrials

Although the vast majority of scientists do not believe that aliens are visiting Earth in spaceships, a hefty proportion of these scientists do think it is possible that extraterrestrial life exists somewhere in the universe. Some scientists are so confident that such life exists, in fact, that they are devoting much time and energy to searching for it. This includes both primitive life and sentient beings as or more advanced than humans. On the one hand, NASA is presently readying probes to look for microbes or other lower life-forms in the outer regions of the solar system. On the other, sophisticated searches for signals from advanced alien races are ongoing. These searches fall under the general heading of SETI, which stands for the Search for Extraterrestrial Intelligence.

The discovery of microbes or other simple life-forms on Mars, Europa, or other bodies in the solar system would certainly be big news and alter the way many people view the universe. In contrast, finding evidence of sentient extraterrestrials would be much more dramatic. And actual communication, including an exchange of information, with such beings would have profound effects on humanity. According to Carl Sagan and Joseph Shklovskii:

> If we were to succeed in establishing contact with an extraterrestrial civilization, especially one possessing a high degree of scientific development, the impact on our lives, our society, and our philosophical outlook would be incalculable.[47]

The reason scientists are so sure that contact with sentient aliens will have so great an impact is that it is virtually

An artist's conception of a giant city on an alien world. Beings capable of erecting such structures would be able to signal other civilizations.

certain such communication will be with a civilization more advanced than our own. University of California geochemist Alan E. Rubin explains:

> Because we have been capable of sending radio transmissions across the galaxy for only a few decades, if we receive an alien signal from a star more than, say, 100 light-years away, it would mean that the alien broadcasters were technologically more advanced than we were when the signal was transmitted. Given the billions of years available for life to have evolved in the galaxy, it is extremely improbable that civilizations on different planets would reach the same technological level at the same time. If there are relatively few technological civilizations in the galaxy . . . these societies would tend to be widely separated both in space and in technological sophistication. Because we could not detect a civilization significantly less technologically advanced than our own (they would lack radio), the odds are [that] any signal we do receive would have been sent by a technologically more advanced society. Unintentional leakage from domestic alien broadcasts would probably be of low power and difficult to detect. Thus, if we ever acquire an alien radio signal, it is likely to be an intentional beacon.[48]

Ongoing Searches for Alien Life

No such beacons have been detected from within the solar system, nor do scientists expect any to appear. This is because they believe that any life that may exist on nearby planets and moons will be non-sentient and likely fairly primitive. The search for life in the solar system began in earnest when NASA landed two spacecraft—Viking 1 and Viking 2—on Mars in 1976. These probes collected soil samples and analyzed them in small portable onboard labs.

They found no conclusive evidence for life on the Martian surface, but a number of scientists remain optimistic that microbes or simple multicelled creatures may later be found living deep underground. The Jet Propulsion Lab in Pasadena, California, has designed specialized robots to dig deep into the Martian soil. These will be aboard spacecraft that will land on the red planet in upcoming missions.

Scientists at the Jet Propulsion Lab are also building devices that will search for life in the subsurface seas of Europe, Ganymede, and possibly Triton. Called "cryobots," each is about three feet long and looks something like a torpedo. A spacecraft will go into orbit around Europa. Then, on a signal from NASA scientists on Earth, it will drop a cryobot onto the moon's icy surface, and a heating element in the device's nose will begin melting the ice. The probe will sink deeper and deeper until it reaches the inner ocean. At that point, onboard lights, cameras, and detectors will be activated and begin searching for life.

Though these projects are ambitious and important, their potential payoff is not as great as the one SETI could conceivably deliver. Serious consideration of systematic searches for sentient life beyond the solar system began in the 1950s. It was in that decade that large radio telescopes began to be built. Big antennas shaped like shallow bowls, these instruments collect radio waves and other kinds of invisible radiation emitted naturally by various cosmic objects. It occurred to Italian astronomer Giuseppe Cocconi and American physicist Philip Morrison that radio telescopes could be used to detect artificial signals as well. In 1959 they published a scientific paper advocating such searches, a document now seen as the birth of SETI.

Inspired by Cocconi and Morrison, the following year Frank Drake launched Project Ozma, named after Princess Ozma, a character in the Oz stories of L. Frank Baum. Using the eighty-five-foot-wide radio telescope at the National Radio Astronomy Observatory in Green Bank,

West Virginia, Drake investigated two stars—Tau Ceti and Epsilon Eridani—hoping to find a repeated signal that was unlikely to be natural in origin. He detected nothing unusual. However, Paul Davies points out, "The project served to focus attention on the possibility of alien communication and the enormous philosophical consequences that would follow from the success of such a search."[49] Several other short-term searches followed in the United States, Canada, and the Soviet Union.

Full-time searches for extraterrestrial signals began in the early 1980s with the foundation of the SETI Institute in southern California. For about a decade, primary funding for the project came from NASA. In 1994 budgetary problems forced NASA to withdraw its monetary support, forcing SETI scientists to rely on contributions from private organizations. Then a reversal occurred in 2003, when the space agency once more began providing government

A cryobot, designed at the Jet Propulsion Lab, melts its way through a pile of ice in a lab test. Such devices will be used to explore Jupiter's moon Europa.

money for the search for alien civilizations. Today, SETI employs more than 130 scientists, many of them Nobel Prize winners.

Where Is Everybody?

To date, SETI has studied thousands of stars, most of them located in the Sun's general neighborhood, and so far no confirmed alien signals of any kind have been detected. Does this silence indicate that sentient extraterrestrials do not exist? "Where is everybody?" Isaac Asimov asks.

> If there were indeed hundreds of millions of advanced civilizations in our galaxy, we should think that they might well have ventured beyond their own worlds; they might have formed alliances; they might have formed a Galactic Federation of Civilizations with emissaries sent to other galactic federations beyond the intergalactic spaces. And, in particular, they should have visited us. Why haven't they?[50]

SETI personnel typically answer such queries by reminding people that only a tiny fraction of stars in the Milky Way—less than one-tenth of 1 percent—have been investigated so far. This is hardly a representative sampling, they say, and it may take centuries to look at them all.

Also, some SETI researchers and other scientists caution that, no matter how hard humans may search, it is possible that no alien signal will be found. However, they add, that would still not mean that no sentient extraterrestrials are out there. Indeed, there are numerous reasons why aliens might not be able, or perhaps might not want, to reveal their presence. The case has been made, for instance, that the vast distances between stars and galaxies may make interstellar travel too difficult and costly for most sentient races. If so, says Asimov:

Either One or Many Alien Civilizations

In this tract from *Are We Alone?* philosopher Paul Davies suggests that humanity is either alone in the universe or one of many sentient extraterrestrial races.

The discovery of a single alien signal from a location somewhere in our galaxy would imply more than the existence of one other civilization. If civilizations are so improbable that only two exist in the entire observable universe, the probability that both would occur in the Milky-Way galaxy is exceedingly small. Therefore we could assume that many other civilizations exist (or have existed, or will exist) in other galaxies. Similarly, if we were to detect a signal as a result of a limited search in our galactic neighborhood, it would imply that civilizations were common throughout the galaxy. It seems that either we are alone in the universe or intelligent life is fairly widespread.

Is humanity a lonely island in the vastness of space, or one of many sentient races?

the vast majority of civilizations, conceivably all of them, may simply remain in their own planetary systems. Any interstellar probes that are sent out may be devices not designed to land on habitable planets but to confine themselves to observations and reports from space. . . . In this way, we can rationalize the apparent paradox that while the galaxy may be rich in civilizations, we remain unaware of them.[51]

Simple timing may also be a crucial factor. It is possible that humans are among the first sentient species to create technological civilizations in the galaxy. In that case, other races may not have had time to develop either the means of interstellar travel or the devices needed to send electronic signals to the stars. Remember that humans developed such capabilities only in the last half-century. And even if some smart aliens *have* developed high technology, perhaps they have legal, religious, or other taboos about using it in the ways we do. Or maybe they are afraid to reveal their presence, fearing an invasion from space. It is also possible that they simply have no interest whatsoever in space.

Other hypotheses have been proposed to explain why extraterrestrials, if they do exist, have not yet made contact.

Frank Drake stands beneath the grid of a radio telescope. Drake has been the leading figure in the SETI program.

One suggests that one or more space-faring alien races *have* discovered humanity's existence. But they consider human beings to be somehow odd or inferior and have set aside Earth and its vicinity as a sort of cosmic zoo or game preserve; in this situation, the aliens are allowed to observe and study humans all they want, but contact is forbidden.

A related but less arrogant and manipulative situation is sometimes referred to as the quarantine hypothesis. It suggests that advanced races believe it is unethical to interfere in the internal affairs of other cultures until those cultures reach a certain level of development. This is the basis for the well-known "prime directive" in the *Star Trek* universe. Federation vessels are allowed to observe developing civilizations from a discreet distance but must be careful not to reveal their presence until the natives develop the means of traveling beyond their home star systems.

Survival in a Hostile Universe

Still another reason that contact with alien civilizations may rarely or never happen is related to the longevity of such civilizations. It may be that many or even most sentient races do not survive long enough to develop large-scale, far-reaching interstellar communication or exploration. After all, even when life does take hold on a planet, there are no guarantees that it will continue to survive. Perhaps some and even most races inevitably destroy themselves with nuclear or other devastating weapons. "If civilizations destroy themselves rapidly after reaching the technological phase," Sagan writes,

> at any given moment (like now) there may be very few of them for us to contact. If, on the other hand, a small fraction of civilizations learn to live with weapons of mass destruction and avoid . . . self-generated catastrophes, the number of civilizations for us to communicate with at any given moment may be very large.[52]

It is also possible that many of those civilizations that do learn to avoid self-annihilation may not survive the effects of much larger cosmic disasters. Indeed, though they are tough and resilient, Earth's ecosystems and life-forms enjoy what is in reality a precarious existence. Small-to-medium-size meteors impact the planet all the time. And periodically, larger asteroids and comets strike, causing enormous explosions that can wipe out cities or, on occasion, cause mass extinctions. Even if such a catastrophe

A dinosaur is startled by the crash of the asteroid (or comet) destined to wipe out more than 70 percent of Earth's plant and animals species.

does not destroy all life on a planet, it can still wipe out any intelligent beings that might have evolved there.

On the flip side, it can be argued that such beings might actually evolve *as a result* of a major cosmic catastrophe. In fact, this is exactly what happened on Earth. An asteroid or comet about six miles across struck the planet 65 million years ago, killing more than 70 percent of all plant and animal species, including all of the dinosaurs. This allowed mammals, culminating in humans, to become the dominant life-forms on Earth. However, as Rubin explains, this outcome is only one of many possible ones resulting from such a disaster and should be seen more as a lucky break (for humans at least) than the norm:

> Such events are very random, could happen at any time, and will not happen the same way even under identical conditions. The demise of the dinosaurs opened up fresh opportunities for mammals and

allowed them to diversify. Without this impact there would have been no cows, cats, pigs, or people. If, however, Earth's clock were turned back and history started anew, the catastrophic impact would surely not have come 65 million years ago; it might not have come at all, or it might have come before mammals had evolved. There may even have been a second impact tens of millions of years later that wiped out most of the mammals. It is also possible that a large projectile would have collided with the Earth 65 million years ago and caused the extinction of all multi-cellular organisms.[53]

Ranking Technological Civilizations

Before his untimely death in 1996, Carl Sagan suggested that the longevity of a sentient civilization might be closely related to the level of complexity of its technology. In other words, those races that lack the technology to fend off ice ages, cosmic impacts, exploding stars, and other such disasters are likely to become extinct sooner or later; whereas

A planet killer like this asteroid zeroed in on Earth 65 million years ago. If this disaster had not occurred, humans would probably not have evolved.

those civilizations that manage to develop the technology to protect themselves from such threats might endure for millions or even billions of years. Sagan was convinced that at least one such ancient race (and perhaps several) might exist in the Milky Way. And logically, this is the one that humans will end up contacting or will eventually end up contacting humans.

But "advanced" is a rather general term. Just how advanced must a civilization become to be able to survive so long? And what are the criteria humans can use to categorize the levels of advancement of alien civilizations and thereby narrow the search for them? Sagan and those who agree with him classify alien technological civilizations according to a scheme developed in 1964 by Russian physicist Nikolai Kardashev. Kardashev ranked such civilizations according to their ability to harness a given, measurable amount of energy. "Because energy, by definition, is the 'ability to work,'" says noted physicist Michio Kaku,

> civilizations could be quickly organized according to their output, for example, in simple universal units such as horsepower. Kardashev's analysis is particularly useful given that the successive stages of human history can likewise be ranked according to energy assets, from prehistoric times (when we only possessed the power of our hands, about one-fifth of a horsepower), to slavery (when kings had hundreds of horsepower at their disposal), to feudalism (thousands of horsepower), to the industrial revolution (millions of horsepower), and finally to modern times (billions of horsepower).[54]

In a similar manner, Kardashev envisioned three basic levels of sentient technology. The first, which he called a Type I civilization, is able to harness and use the entire potential energy output of a planet. At present, humanity

If humanity becomes a Type I civilization, it will likely be capable of building twenty-mile-wide floating space cities like this one.

still has Type 0 status on the scale. This is because humans still derive most of their energy from crude means such as burning coal, oil, and other fossil fuels. Only when they unlock the energy reserves of wind, solar, geothermal, and fusion power on a global scale will they fully exploit the planet's potential. Some scientists, including renowned Princeton University scholar Freeman Dyson, think that, barring some unforeseen catastrophe, humanity may reach Type I status within two centuries or so.

A Type II civilization on Kardashev's scale is one that has learned to tap the energy output of a single star such as the Sun. The Sun's output is huge, to be sure—up to 100 billion trillion horsepower at any given moment. But how could a race of beings manage to capture so much radiant energy? Several years ago Dyson proposed that they might erect an immense sphere around the star. This "Dyson sphere," as it has come to called, need not be solid, but could consist of billions of orbiting cities and energy-collecting satellites. Such a sphere might be invisible to Earth's searching eyes and telescopes; but its heat output would leak out into space in the form of infrared radiation, which humans might be able to detect.

A Type III civilization, according to Kardashev, would be able to harness the energy output of an entire galaxy. These, says Kaku, are the most promising aliens for SETI searchers

> because they possess the greatest capacity for achieving immortality. Ice ages can be altered, meteorites can be deflected, and even supernovas [exploding stars] or gamma-ray bursters [cosmic outbursts of deadly radiation] will damage [only] a small part of a Type III civilization. Once a Type III civilization evolves in a galaxy, it should last for millions or even billions of years. . . . This led Carl Sagan and others to speculate that a Type III civilization may exist within the Milky Way.[55]

Profound Implications of Contact

What would the impact of contact with such a civilization be on human society? There is no doubt that humanity's outlook on the universe, as well as its material opportunities for both the present and the future, would be fundamentally altered. This assumes, of course, that the aliens are altruistic—that is, benevolent and unselfish about sharing what they know. As Seth Shostak, points out, this may or may not be the case:

> Although the extraterrestrials would probably be altruistic with one another . . . that possibility alone says very little about whether they would be "moral" with us. Altruism has a biological basis. . . . A selfless act may prompt reciprocity [giving in return] at a later date. One good deed encourages another, and both the individual and the species benefit. However, when it comes to interactions between extraterrestrials and humans, the aliens will have

little biological reason to be altruistic, only intellectual ones. After all, consider how we treat animals. Some are our pets. Others we grind up and lace with ketchup. Human attitudes about the treatment of our local "aliens," namely animals, are highly divergent. We treat many of these other species badly (from their point of view). Why shouldn't the aliens behave the same way towards *their* aliens? This argument might be faulted on the grounds that the animals we abuse are, after all, not terribly intellectual. Presumably, any ET in contact with us will recognize our cognitive horsepower, and grant us a little respect. We're all sentient beings, after all, and surely we can sympathize with one another?[56]

Following this reasoning, Alan E. Rubin postulates that "an ancient, advanced civilization may even feel obligated to aid struggling newcomers to the galactic community with helpful advice on such topics as increasing agricultural productivity, avoiding nuclear war, [and] eliminating pollution."[57]

Thus, assuming the advanced aliens *are* altruistic and willing to have a relationship with humanity, they will likely share their accumulated knowledge, or at least some of it, with humans. They might do so via electronic signals like those SETI seeks, or they may send robotic probes carrying the information. They might also come in person. If they are thousands or millions of years ahead of us in science, they will have developed the means of producing abundant energy; and as Rubin has pointed out, their methods will not pollute the environment. These methods may include nuclear fusion (the same process that drives a hydrogen bomb, except safely controlled), capturing the energy output of stars (with Dyson spheres or other means), or even manipulating black holes (super-dense objects having truly enormous energy potentials).

Acquiring such technology would allow humans to eliminate poverty, disease, and other large-scale problems almost overnight. Indeed, there would easily be enough energy to support the spread of billions of people into cities floating in space or even to terraform (create Earth-like conditions on) planets whose environments are presently hostile to Earth life.

Advances in science and technological prowess would also profoundly change people's everyday lives. The mini-

Although most distant alien civilizations will probably communicate via electronic signals, a few may come in person , as did the fictional E.T.

mum standard of living for people everywhere would conceivably be high and comfortable. In that case, average workweeks would be significantly shorter and every home would be equipped with laborsaving devices. People would have much more free time available for educational pursuits, social activities, political involvement, travel, and entertainment. New and better ways of growing, preserving, and storing food might eliminate hunger and allow everyone access to more diverse foods. And human communications abilities may well leap far ahead of their present state. Movies could become completely three-dimensional and, when desired, interactive. And solid-looking three-dimensional images of people could be projected anywhere, so a person and the distant friends and business associates he or she calls would all appear to be sitting together in the same room.

On the other hand, perhaps the beings in question will be so advanced that they will have outgrown the need for normal physical bodies and technology. Some scientists and writers have explored the idea that the continued evolution of intelligence might occasionally lead to beings who consist of pure energy (or intellect) rather than flesh and blood. Arthur C. Clarke explored this concept brilliantly and hauntingly in *2001: A Space Odyssey*. In the story, human astronaut Dave Bowman is completely befuddled and intimidated by the super-beings (until he is reborn as one of them in the climax). This is an example of Clarke's famous maxim—that any race sufficiently advanced over humans will be indistinguishable from magic. Such beings may well be equally indistinguishable from what humans see as gods.

Of Gods, Men, and Aliens

Despite whether humanity sees such advanced aliens as gods, the discovery of sentient extraterrestrials will almost surely impact the way people view and understand themselves, their social customs, and their place in the universe.

Concepts of nationality, race, gender roles, religious beliefs, and so forth would surely be reexamined in new light.

There is the possibility, for example, that the aliens in a Type III civilization might significantly influence Earth's religions. These beings may feel that they have found the true meaning of spirituality or that they are closer to God than members of less-advanced civilizations. If so, they may dismiss human religious ideas and urge people to think and worship as they do. "Convinced that they have found the one true religion," Rubin suggests, these beings "might broadcast a message to save the souls of intelligent beings throughout the galaxy. It could be an alien version of . . . Matthew 28:19 [in the Bible]. 'Go ye therefore and teach all nations.'"[58] Not all humans would respond to such cosmic evangelism, of course; but some would undoubtedly form new religions based on that of the aliens. On the other hand, these advanced extraterrestrials might claim that they have evolved beyond the need for religion. If so, such a statement coming from such an awe-inspiring source would affect the spiritual thinking of at least some of Earth's inhabitants.

It is possible, of course, that no Type III civilizations exist, at least in our galaxy. Maybe there are only Type I and II civilizations. Or perhaps the only extraterrestrial life in the universe consists of slime molds and worms. What is certain is that the human mind is curious, restless, and compelled to know if living things are waiting to be found in the vast gulfs of interstellar space. So, ongoing searches for extraterrestrial life will continue. Most scientists feel that, given enough time, such inquiries will reveal whether extraterrestrial life is common or rare. "The technological hurdles for these projects are formidable," says Australian astronomer R. Paul Butler,

> and it is difficult to predict when any of them
> might see fruition. But the questions they may

How did the universe form? What role will humanity play in the destiny of the universe? Contact with more advanced beings may help answer such questions.

answer are no less profound. What is our place in the universe? Are there other Earths? Is our heart-warming solar system a freakish twist in the cosmic script or merely some common plot device used over and over? . . . We do not know—but we will.[59]

Notes

Introduction: ETs in History and the Imagination

1. H.G. Wells, *The War of the Worlds*. 1898. Reprint, New York: Berkley, 1964, p. 7.

2. Paul Davies, *Are We Alone? Philosophical Implications of the Discovery of Extraterrestrial Life*. New York: BasicBooks, 1995, p. 12.

3. Quoted in Clifford Pickover, *The Science of Aliens*. New York: BasicBooks, 1998, p. 13.

4. Quoted in Diogenes Laertius, *Lives of Eminent Philosophers*, vol. 2, trans. R.D. Hicks. Cambridge, MA: Harvard University Press, 1995, pp. 575, 605.

5. Isaac Asimov, *Extraterrestrial Civilizations*. New York: Fawcett, 1980, p. 24.

6. Quoted in Davies, *Are We Alone?* pp. 5–6.

7. Thomas Paine, *The Age of Reason*. 1774. Reprint, Buffalo: Prometheus, 1984, p. 280.

8. Davies, *Are We Alone?* p. xii.

Chapter One: How Likely or Common Is Extraterrestrial Life?

9. Frank Drake, *Is Anyone Out There?* New York: Delacorte, 1992, p. 7.

10. Davies, *Are We Alone?* p. 13.

11. Davies, *Are We Alone?* p. 13.

12. Joe Alper, "It Came from Outer Space," *Astronomy*, November 2002, pp. 38–39.

13. Quoted in Alper, "It Came from Outer Space," p. 36.

14. Terence Dickinson and Adolf Schaller, *Extraterrestrials: A Field Guide for Earthlings*. Ontario: Camden House, 1994, p. 19.

15. Dana Mackenzie, "Is There Life Under the Ice?" *Astronomy*, August 2001, p. 35.

16. Quoted in J. Kelly Beatty et al., *The New Solar System*. Cambridge, UK: Cambridge University Press, 1999, p. 369.

17. Mackenzie, "Is There Life Under the Ice?" p. 35.

18. Quoted in Robert Naeye, "An Ocean for Ganymede, Too," *Astronomy*, May 2001, p. 26.

19. Actually, in 1992 some planets had purportedly been found orbiting a super-dense object called a neutron star. But these were hard to confirm; and in any case, astronomers did not consider them to be part of a normal planetary system.

20. Carl Sagan and I.S. Shklovskii, *Intelligent Life in the Universe*. Garden City, NY: Doubleday, 1980, p. 418.

21. Davies, *Are We Alone?* p. 64.

22. Quoted in Beatty et al., *The New Solar System*, p. 369.

23. Pickover, *The Science of Aliens*, pp. 191–92.

Chapter Two: What Physical Forms Might Extraterrestrials Have?

24. Dickinson and Schaller, *Extraterrestrials*, p. 7.

25. Quoted in Ben Zuckerman and Michael H. Hart, eds., *Extraterrestrials: Where Are They?* New York: Cambridge University Press, 1995, pp. 165, 167.

26. Quoted in Pickover, *The Science of Aliens*, p. 13.

27. Pickover, *The Science of Aliens*, p. 19.

28. Dickinson and Schaller, *Extraterrestrials*, pp. 36–37.

29. Pickover, *The Science of Aliens*, pp. 86–87.

30. Sagan and Shklovskii, *Intelligent Life in the Universe*, p. 351.

31. Pickover, *The Science of Aliens*, pp. 52–53.

32. Dickinson and Schaller, *Extraterrestrials*, p. 28.

33. Seth Shostak, *Sharing the Universe: Perspectives on Extraterrestrial Life*. Berkeley, CA: Berkeley Hills, 1998, p. 75.

34. Dickinson and Schaller, *Extraterrestrials*, p. 31.

35. Quoted in Zuckerman and Hart, *Extraterrestrials*, pp. 167–68.

36. Quoted in Zuckerman and Hart, *Extraterrestrials*, p. 168.

37. Pickover, *The Science of Aliens*, p. 62.

38. Pickover, *The Science of Aliens*, p. 194.

Chapter Three: Are Extraterrestrial Spacecraft Visiting Earth?

39. Isaac Asimov, *Is Anyone There?* New York: Ace Books, 1980, p. 216.

40. Asimov, *Extraterrestrial Civilizations*, p. 202.

41. Quoted in Zuckerman and Hart, *Extraterrestrials*, pp. 23–24.

42. Shostak, *Sharing the Universe*, pp. 42–43.

43. Asimov, *Is Anyone There?* p. 216.

44. Curtis Peebles, *Watch the Skies! A Chronicle of the Flying Saucer Myth.* Washington, DC: Smithsonian Institution, 1994, pp. 290–91.

45. Shostak, *Sharing the Universe*, p. 5.

46. Carl Sagan, *The Cosmic Connection: An Extraterrestrial Perspective.* New York: Dell, 1973, p. 43.

Chapter Four: The Ongoing Search for Sentient Extraterrestrials

47. Sagan and Shklovskii, *Intelligent Life in the Universe*, p. 380.

48. Alan E. Rubin, *Disturbing the Solar System: Impacts, Close Encounters, and Coming Attractions.* Princeton, NJ: Princeton University Press, 2002, p. 300.

49. Davies, *Are We Alone?* p. 16.

50. Asimov, *Extraterrestrial Civilizations*, pp. 177–78.

51. Asimov, *Extraterrestrial Civilizations*, p. 249.

52. Sagan, *The Cosmic Connection*, p. 35.

53. Rubin, *Disturbing the Solar System*, p. 293.

54. Michio Kaku, "Who Will Inherit the Universe?" *Astronomy*, February 2002, p. 36.

55. Kaku, "Who Will Inherit the Universe?" p. 37.

56. Shostak, *Sharing the Universe*, pp. 100–101.

57. Rubin, *Disturbing the Solar System*, p. 305.

58. Rubin, *Disturbing the Solar System*, p. 304.

59. Quoted in Beatty et al., *The New Solar System*, p. 386.

Glossary

abductee: A person who claims he or she has been abducted by extraterrestrial beings.

accretion: A process in which clumps of material stick together, forming a larger clump.

amino acids: Organic compounds found in proteins, the building blocks of living tissue.

ammonia: A colorless, poisonous gas made up of the elements nitrogen and hydrogen.

aquatic: Water-based; living in the ocean.

asteroid: A small stony or metallic body orbiting the sun, most often in the asteroid belt lying between the planets Mars and Jupiter.

bilateral symmetry: A physical characteristic in which the limbs, eyes, ears, and other body parts on the left side of an imaginary line drawn down the middle of a creature look the same as those on the right side. Humans, birds, fish, and insects are all bilaterally symmetrical.

biochemical: Having to do with the chemicals that make up living things.

contactee: A person who claims that he or she has made personal contact with extraterrestrial beings.

Dyson sphere: A huge shell constructed around a star with the purpose of capturing and exploiting the star's energy.

electromagnetic spectrum: The range of different kinds of visible and invisible radiation, including visual light, ultraviolet light, X rays, radio waves, and others.

extrasolar: Existing beyond the solar system.

extraterrestrial (ET): A living thing originating from beyond Earth.

extremophiles: Living things that exist and thrive in environments that are harsh, poisonous, or otherwise extreme for humans and most other Earth creatures.

galaxy: A gigantic group of stars held together by their combined gravities. Our galaxy is called the Milky Way.

gravity: A force exerted by an object that attracts other objects. The pull of Earth's gravity keeps rocks, trees, people, and houses from floating away into space. It also holds the Moon in orbit around Earth.

habitable zone: The region in a star system

in which liquid water can exist on planetary surfaces, providing a friendly environment for the development of life.

humanoid: Having a general shape similar to that of humans (i.e., a head, torso, two arms, and two legs).

interstellar: Between stars, usually referring to travel from one star to another.

light-year: The distance that light travels in a year, or about 6 trillion miles.

NASA: The National Aeronautics and Space Administration, the official U.S. government agency in charge of learning about and exploring the universe.

neutron star: A super-dense object made up almost entirely of neutrons (subatomic particles with no electrical charge); a neutron star forms from the catastrophic collapse of a large star and has crushing gravity.

Occam's razor (or the principle of parsimony): A scientific rule of thumb that advocates that one should not turn to an extraordinary explanation for an unknown phenomenon until all ordinary ones have been conclusively eliminated.

orbit: To move around something; or the path taken by a planet, comet, or asteroid around the Sun or a moon around a planet.

organic materials: Substances making up the building blocks of living things.

organism: A plant, animal, or other living thing.

planetesimals: Small objects that orbited the early Sun and combined to form the planets, moons, asteroids, and comets.

radio telescope: A large bowl-shaped antenna designed to collect radio waves and other kinds of electromagnetic radiation.

sentient: Having enough intelligence to be conscious, self-aware, and capable of creating a technical civilization.

SETI: The Search for Extraterrestrial Intelligence; a collection of programs organized to seek out signals from alien civilizations.

solar system: The Sun and all of the objects that orbit it.

sonar: Invisible waves sent out by a machine or an animal (such as a dolphin); the waves strike objects and bounce back, revealing the position and shape of the objects.

stellar: Having to do with stars.

thermal: Having to do with heat.

Type I civilization: A civilization with the capability of harnessing the energy output of a planet.

Type II civilization: A civilization with the capability of harnessing the energy output of a star.

Type III civilization: A civilization with the capability of harnessing the energy output of a galaxy.

UFO: Unidentified Flying Object; an object one sees in the sky but is unable to identify; the term is often used interchangeably with "flying saucer," referring to a piloted alien spacecraft.

universe: The sum total of all the space and matter known to exist.

For Further Reading

For Beginning and Intermediate Readers

Books

Nigel Henbest, *DK Space Encyclopedia*. London: Dorling Kindersley, 1999. This beautifully mounted and critically acclaimed book is the best general source available for grade-school readers about the wonders of space.

Jacqueline Mitton, *Aliens*. Cambridge, MA: Candlewick, 1999. The author explains that, with the exception of that on Earth, intelligent life is not likely to exist in our solar system, but that it may exist around other stars. She also tells about SETI, the search for signals from alien civilizations.

Sally Ride and Tam O'Shaughnessy, *The Mystery of Mars*. New York: Crown, 1999. A commendable exploration of the red planet, the book compares Mars to Earth, discusses the possibility of life on Mars, and tells about the various space missions that have explored that planet.

Philip Wilkerson et al., *Invaders from Outer Space*. London: Dorling Kindersley, 1999. A fascinating overview of possible visitations of Earth by extraterrestrials.

Internet Sources

NASA, "The Shape of Extraterrestrial Life." http://science.nasa.gov. Explores the use of artificial intelligence to search for extraterrestrial life.

UFO Alliance, "Extraterrestrial Life and UFOs." www.webpan.com. A large, informative site providing many links to articles about the possible existence of extraterrestrial life and the visitation of the Earth by aliens.

For More Advanced Readers and/or Science-Fiction Buffs

The author highly recommends the following well-written and absorbing science-fiction works about human contact with alien civilizations. All deal in a realistic manner with the scientific principles and possibilities involved and are considered classics in the genre:

Isaac Asimov, *The Gods Themselves*. New York: Fawcett-Crest, 1972. Asimov's award-winning depiction of intelligent beings living in a universe normally beyond human perception.

Isaac Asimov et al., eds., *Flying Saucers*. New York: Fawcett-Crest, 1982. A collection of some of the best-ever short stories about piloted UFOs.

Greg Bear, *The Forge of God*. New York: Tom Doherty, 1987. A suspenseful, grandly told tale of a sinister alien race out to destroy Earth.

Arthur C. Clarke, *Childhood's End*. New York: Ballantine, 1953. Clarke's best novel and indeed one of the greatest novels ever written, this deals with the frightening consequences when Earth encounters a super-mentality whose long-term goals include the elimination of the human race.

———, *2001: A Space Odyssey*. New York: New American Library, 1968. Clarke's famous tale of human astronauts finding an alien artifact on the Moon and one man's life-altering encounter with the advanced race that planted the artifact.

———, *2010: Odyssey Two*. New York: Ballantine, 1982. Clarke's sequel to *2001* is even better than the original. A suspenseful, thought-provoking encounter with alien super-intelligence.

Hal Clement, *Mission of Gravity*. New York: Del Rey, 1979. This wonderfully intuitive yarn about human astronauts making contact with caterpillar-like beings on a planet with crushing gravity is a fun read from start to finish.

Fred Hoyle, *The Black Cloud*. New York:

New American Library, 1957. Hoyle, one of the twentieth century's greatest astronomers, delivers a fascinating exploration of the possibility of intelligence manifesting itself in interstellar gas clouds.

Larry Niven and Jerry Pournelle, *Footfall*. New York: Ballantine, 1985. A tremendously imaginative and entertaining twist on the alien invasion theme, with many memorable characters, both human and alien.

———, *The Mote in God's Eye*. New York: Pocket, 1974. Set in the year 3016, this is the story of humans expanding outward into the galaxy. Eventually, they encounter a nonhuman sentient race, which welcomes them. But these beings harbor a dark secret. A real page-turner.

Carl Sagan, *Contact*. New York: Simon and Schuster, 1985. A female scientist-astronaut utilizes wormholes to make contact with an advanced civilization. Contains many fascinating futuristic scientific concepts and suggests how humans may come to deal with them.

H.G. Wells, *The War of the Worlds*. 1898. Reprint, New York: Berkley, 1964. The first great classic of alien invasion and still one of the best.

John Wyndham, *Chocky*. New York: Ballantine, 1968. A very offbeat and haunting tale of a young man whose brain channels the thoughts of an alien being.

Jim Wynorski, ed., *They Came from Outer Space*. Garden City, NY: Doubleday, 1980. A collection of twelve classic tales of alien contact, including "Who Goes There?" the basis for both movie versions of *The Thing*.

Major Works Consulted

Isaac Asimov, *Extraterrestrial Civilizations.* New York: Fawcett, 1980. Slightly dated but still one of the best general discussions of the subject, including a great deal of technical information presented in an easy-to-read manner.

J. Kelly Beatty et al., *The New Solar System.* Cambridge, UK: Cambridge University Press, 1999. One of the best available general guides to ongoing knowledge and discoveries in planetary science, including valuable information about possible life on Mars, Europa, and elsewhere in the solar system.

John Billingham et al., eds., *Social Implications of Detection of an Extraterrestrial Intelligence.* Mountain View, CA: SETI, 1999. A collection of essays by experts, each covering one or more ways that human society may react to the discovery of alien beings.

Paul Davies, *Are We Alone? Philosophical Implications of the Discovery of Extraterrestrial Life.* New York: BasicBooks, 1995. An extremely thoughtful and well-written excursion into the realm of ET life and how its discovery will affect human thought and endeavors. Highly recommended.

Terence Dickinson and Adolf Schaller, *Extraterrestrials: A Field Guide for Earthlings.* Ontario: Camden House, 1994. Beautifully illustrated with numerous color drawings and paintings of hypothetical aliens, this volume also has a first-rate (though brief) text. A good starting point for those who are unfamiliar with the subject.

Bill Fawcett, ed., *Making Contact: A Serious Handbook for Locating and Communicating with Extraterrestrials.* New York: William Morrow, 1997. A lucid, well-informed discussion of SETI and other attempts to find ET life, along with some practical ideas for creating dialogues with alien races.

Curtis Peebles, *Watch the Skies! A Chronicle of the Flying Saucer Myth.* Washington, DC: Smithsonian Institution, 1994. Meticulously researched, well organized, detailed, and informative, this is the best available history of the flying saucer/UFO phenomenon. Peebles documents the way the phenomenon has changed over the years directly in response to changes in society and popular culture. A must for those interested in this subject.

Clifford Pickover, *The Science of Aliens.* New

York: BasicBooks, 1998. A fact-filled, imaginative, and fascinating discussion of alien life and the possible physical forms it could take. Superior of its kind.

Alan E. Rubin, *Disturbing the Solar System: Impacts, Close Encounters, and Coming Attractions.* Princeton, NJ: Princeton University Press, 2002. An eclectic but highly informative and entertaining book about the known celestial objects and the mysteries of outer space, including the possibility of extraterrestrial life.

Carl Sagan and I.S. Shklovskii, *Intelligent Life in the Universe.* Garden City, NY: Doubleday, 1980. Long the classic work in the genre, this somewhat scholarly book by two noted scientists is slightly dated but still very comprehensive and well worth the effort.

Seth Shostak, *Sharing the Universe: Perspectives on Extraterrestrial Life.* Berkeley, CA: Berkeley Hills, 1998. An excellent discussion of the probability that alien life exists, the abilities and behavior of such beings, and present efforts to contact sentient races.

Ben Zuckerman and Michael H. Hart, eds., *Extraterrestrials: Where Are They?* New York: Cambridge University Press, 1995. A collection of essays, mostly by scientists who are skeptical about the existence of extraterrestrial intelligence. Many of the discussions are technical and dense and will appeal mainly to scientists and scholars.

Additional Works Consulted

Books

Joseph Angelo, *The Extraterrestrial Encyclopedia: Man's Search for Life in Outer Space.* New York: Facts On File, 1991.

Thomas T. Arny, *Explorations: An Introduction to Astronomy.* New York: McGraw-Hill, 2001.

Isaac Asimov, *Is Anyone There?* New York: Ace Books, 1980.

Ben Bova and Byron Preiss, eds., *First Contact: The Search for Extraterrestrial Intelligence.* New York: New American Library, 1990.

Stuart Clark, *Life on Other Worlds and How to Find It.* London: Springer-Praxis, 2000.

Ken Croswell, *Planet Quest: The Epic Discovery of Alien Solar Systems.* New York: Free Press, 1997.

Steven Dick, *Plurality of Worlds: The Extraterrestrial Life Debate from Democritus to Kant.* New York: Cambridge University Press, 1982.

Frank Drake, *Is Anyone Out There?* New York: Delacorte, 1992.

Paul Halpern, *The Quest for Alien Planets: Exploring Worlds Outside the Solar System.* New York: Plenum, 1997.

Philip J. Klass, *UFO Abductions: A Dangerous Game.* Buffalo: Prometheus, 1989.

———, *UFOs Explained.* New York: Random House, 1974.

Diogenes Laertius, *Lives of Eminent Philosophers.* 2 vols. Trans. R.D. Hicks. Cambridge, MA: Harvard University Press, 1995.

John F. Moffitt, *Picturing Extraterrestrials: Alien Images in Modern Mass Culture.* Amherst, NY: Prometheus, 2003.

Thomas Paine, *The Age of Reason.* 1774. Reprint, Buffalo: Prometheus, 1984.

Carl Sagan, *The Cosmic Connection: An Extraterrestrial Perspective.* New York: Dell, 1973.

Periodicals

Joe Alper, "It Came from Outer Space," *Astronomy*, November 2002.

R.N. Bracewell, "Communications from Superior Galactic Communities," *Nature*, vol. 186, 1960.

Jack Cohen, "How to Design an Alien," *New Scientist*, December 21, 1991.

Mark A. Garlick, "No Place Like Zone," *Astronomy*, August 2002.

Michio Kaku, "Who Will Inherit the Universe?" *Astronomy*, February 2002.

Michael D. Lemonick, "Can We Find Another Earth?" *Discover*, March 2002.

Jeffery M. Lichtman, "Radio Astronomy and Other Civilizations," *Satellite Times*, January/February 1995.

Dana Mackenzie, "Is There Life Under the Ice?" *Astronomy*, August 2001.

Alan M. MacRobert and Joshua Roth, "The Planet of 51 Pegasi," *Sky and Telescope*, January 1996.

Robert Naeye, "Astronomers Probe Alien Skies," *Astronomy*, March 2002.

———, "An Ocean for Ganymede, Too," *Astronomy*, May 2001.

———, "A Planetary System Like Our Own?" *Astronomy*, October 2001.

Ted Peters, "Exo-Theology: Speculations on Extraterrestrial Life," *CTNS Bulletin*, vol. 14, 1994.

Carl Sagan, "The Saucerian Cult," *Saturday Review*, August 6, 1966.

Carl Sagan and Frank Drake, "The Search for Extraterrestrial Intelligence," *Scientific American*, May 1975.

William Schomaker, "Cryobot Gets Ready for Space," *Astronomy*, May 2002.

———, "Scientists Probe Life's Early Days," *Astronomy*, November 2001.

Paul H. Shuch, "Searching for Life Among the Stars," *QST*, August 1995.

Richard Talcott, "Search for Earth-like Planets Narrows," *Astronomy*, February 2002.

Vanessa Thomas, "Life-on-Mars Debate Heats Up," *Astronomy*, November 2002.

William S. Weed, "What's Water Got to Do with It?" *Astronomy*, August 2001.

Internet Sources

Christopher B. Jones, "Life as We Don't Know It (Part 1)," June 2000. www.suite101.com.

———, "Life as We Don't Know It (Part 2)," July 2000. www.suite101.com.

———, "Life as We Don't Know It (Part 3)," July 2000. www.suite101.com.

Lunar and Planetary Institute, "On the Question of the Mars Meteorite," 1996. www.lpi.usra.edu.

J.R. Mooneyham, "The Rise and Fall of Star-Faring Civilizations in Our Own Galaxy," October 2002. http://kurellian.tripod.com.

NASA, "The Center for SETI Research," 2003. www.seti-inst.edu.

NASA, "HD70642: A Star with Similar Planets," July 9, 2003. http://antwrp.gsfc.nasa.gov.

NASA, "Life on Other Planets in the Solar System." www.resa.net.

Charles S. Tritt, "Possibilities of Life on Europa," November 2002. http://people.msoe.edu.

Peter Warrington, "The Drake Equation and Extraterrestrial Life, a Brief Overview," 1996. www.u-net.com.

Alexander J. Willman, Princeton University, "Known Planetary Systems," July 2003. www.princeton.edu.

Index

Picture Credits

About the Author

In addition to his acclaimed volumes on ancient civilizations, historian Don Nardo has published several studies of modern scientific discoveries and phenomena. Among these are *Black Holes; Comets and Asteroids; The Extinction of the Dinosaurs; Cloning;* volumes about Pluto, Neptune, and the Moon; and a biography of the noted scientist Charles Darwin. Mr. Nardo lives with his wife, Christine, in Massachusetts.